# Playing Chopsticks

筷子

Dedicated to the kind and generous people of China who welcomed us,
entertained us and helped us discover their country.

筷
子

# Playing Chopsticks

*Travels Through China*

Sally Hammond

Photography by Gordon Hammond

First published in Australia in 2006 by
New Holland Publishers (Australia) Pty Ltd
Sydney • Auckland • London • Cape Town

www.newholland.com.au

14 Aquatic Drive Frenchs Forest NSW 2086 Australia
218 Lake Road Northcote Auckland New Zealand
86 Edgware Road London W2 2EA United Kingdom
80 McKenzie Street Cape Town 8001 South Africa

National Library of Australia Cataloguing-in-Publication Data:
Hammond, Sally.
          Playing chopsticks : travels through China.

     ISBN 1 74110 397 5.

     1. China - Description and travel. 2. Cookery, Chinese.
     I. Title.


     915.1046

Publisher: Fiona Schultz
Managing Editor: Martin Ford
Production controller: Grace Gutwein
Project Editor: Michael McGrath
Designer: Greg Lamont

Cover image and design: Greg Lamont
Printed in Australia by Griffin Press, Adelaide, South Australia

# Contents

## Appendix

筷
子

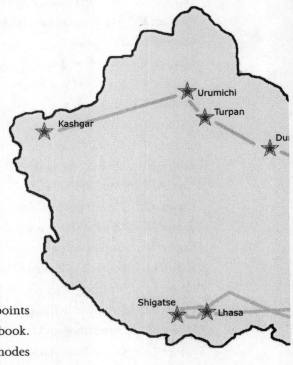

## MAP OF CHINA

These are the major cities and points of interest that feature in this book. We visited them using various modes of transport, including plane, train, bus, car and 4WD.

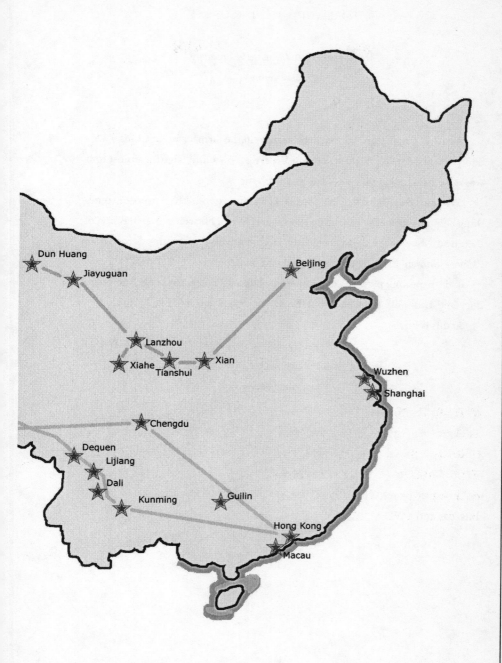

Dun Huang

Jiayuguan

Beijing

Lanzhou

Xiahe
Tianshui

Xian

Wuzhen

Shanghai

Chengdu

Dequen

Lijiang

Dali

Kunming

Guilin

Hong Kong

Macau

筷子

# FOREWORD: PICKING UP

*The palest ink is better than the best memory.*

**Chinese saying**


We are at the airport. Somewhere nearby on the tarmac, an Air China 747 is being readied for our flight to Beijing. We are off on a longish trip, almost four weeks, so I am looking for a book to take with me.

'Why not one about China?' I think. It's always good, I find, to read something about the place we're visiting as we travel. When I search in every section of the airport bookstore there are plenty of epic novels concerning dynasties of Chinese women, but as far as travel stories go, nothing.

In desperation I pick up yet another book about France, pay for it, and board the plane. Looks like I will have to write my own book about China, I think.

So this is it!


*To know the road ahead, ask those coming back.*

**Chinese Proverb**

筷
子

## NOTES FOR THE READER

This is not a guidebook, and is not meant to be a definitive guide, or even an exhaustive exposition. Nor is it a complete travelogue covering any one route or region.

It is, more accurately, a series of reminiscences and anecdotes collected in an attempt to bring China alive for those who have not yet visited, and awaken memories for those who have.

For specific information, use the Internet or ask your travel agent.

**Spelling:** In this book, I have spelt place names as I have seen them converted from Mandarin or Tibetan into pinyin, which is written in the alphabet we use. As there is no exact spelling, these names can vary enormously from book to book or even on signs in the place itself. I have chosen one and stayed with it, but you may find many others as you continue to read about, and visit, this country.

**Names:** For various reasons many of the names of our guides and fellow travellers have been changed. Maybe it's a good idea, anyway. I recently checked an Internet site and discovered my name translates to Hong Xu Lun, while my husband Gordon's is He Ge Rong.

## ACKNOWLEDGMENTS

There are many people who have assisted us in visiting China over the years and I would like to thank them here.

Most notably, Helen Wong from Helen Wong's Tours, has been generous with both her time and her expertise, and in arranging guides and tours for us at various times.

Likewise, Tashi Lachman from Thor Adventure Travel opened our eyes to Tibet and helped us to learn about and love her people there. Cathay Pacific has been helpful and generous too.

To Fiona Schultz, Publisher, New Holland Publishers, many thanks are due for believing in the sketchy outline of this book and commissioning me to write it.

Likewise my editor at New Holland, thank you too for your patience and diligence.

But no acknowledgments would be complete without my deepest thanks to my husband, Gordon, who is my life partner, travelling mate, best friend, photographer extraordinaire, IT support, and all round the finest person to share my work and life with. What's more he wrote a chapter of this book, with his own perspective of photography in China, and supplied the lovely black and white sketch-photos in each chapter, as well as the images for the back cover.

Thank you all!

# 1. SHOP-STICKS

*Don't open a shop unless you like to smile.*
**Chinese Proverb**

On my first morning in China I am called on to declare that I do not have leprosy. I must also state that I have no psychoses, or was that phobias? I want to tell the authorities that I have a pathological fear of filling out forms—does that count?—but am not sure if they'd get the joke!

All of this takes place at 30 000 feet as we fly on the appropriately named Dragon Air from Hong Kong to K'unming, capital of Yunnan province in south-western China. This is before the handover, when HK is still Honkers and under British rule. That flimsy little immigration form seems endless—AIDS? No! Tuberculosis? No. Anxiety? Well ... maybe!

Then there is a choice of strange and creative categories of employment. Too hard. I tick 'worker' and move on. Surely that should do. After all, it has a nice comrade-ish ring to it.

This was all over a decade ago, when red was still much more than a colour in China. You could feel the political climate as readily as the one that's connected to wind and rain. More of that later. On this particular morning high above the clouds, my major emotion is excitement, for we are off to see a country I have explored in my mind all my life. Best of all our ultimate aim is to visit Lhasa, the Forbidden City.

As a child in Australia, dreaming over a school atlas, China was a big blank land. I remember it as pink, but maybe not, because the British Empire had commandeered that hue, painting much of the world with it at that stage. My encyclopaedias showed no pictures of China save for some of rice-field workers in conical coolie hats. They could have been posed in Michigan, for all we knew, because for all my life, and many years before, China had been closed, and only began to open up to the outside world, crack by tiny crack, in the 1970s.

We'd called it the 'bamboo curtain' but it was nothing like the collection of flimsy strips of threaded cane that people hang in doorways to deter insects, screens that you can elbow through with your arms full. For decades this one had been virtually impenetrable to outsiders, except those with a rolled gold excuse (and maybe a roll or two of gold, too).

My in-flight meal arrives—shrimp salad, pork with fried potato balls, and a sensuously silky sesame mousse which I could happily have reordered. How often can you say that about airline food? I check my husband, Gordon's plate. He has noodles and chicken paired with a clump of black fungus. It looks more like haberdashery than something one should chew. Hmmm! I decide to leave that well alone and settle down with my remaining bread roll and glass of French red wine. If this is China, then it is a country I will surely like, I decide.

K'unming lies at an altitude of 1894 metres, and I have good cause to remember this fact later. Tony, our tour guide, in the manner of most of his profession has thrown this and a fistful of other stats at us in those first few minutes on the minibus as we leave the airport. I may not consciously hear it then, but I can tell you the exact point at which I recall it.

An hour later I am labouring up a hill to a temple Tony wants us to see...

筷
子

or is it the palace? I've lost concentration and my breathing is tight and getting tighter. I am falling behind. Just moments before hypochondria sets in (it's a heart attack, I know it!) I realise 'it' is simply the elevation and slow my pace even more.

Although K'unming—with a moderate climate which has earned it the title of 'Spring City' or 'Capital of Flowers'—doesn't quite reach the 2000-metre mark generally regarded as the indicator to take care with altitude, it is close enough, especially when factoring in a long flight and all the excitement of travel.

We're part of a group of twelve people, all bug-eyed with anticipation, hyped with the ultra-observation I've often experienced on Day One in just about every country I have visited, when each nerve ending is primed to absorb the sights and sounds, smells and flavours of a new place.

'You buy, you buy?' people cry out as we pass. 'One dollar, please … you like?'

All the way, there are stalls selling food or ornaments, jade carvings, lucky bits and pieces. I nearly buy a couple of chirping crickets (plastic) in a box as a present but, thankfully, don't. I do buy a necklace, though, which I have never worn (genuine Lucite®, they tell me—which must mean plastic) for 30 yuan near the shrine and wishing well at the temple gates, where you can attempt to lob a coin onto a stone frog's nose for good luck.

Back in the bus parking area the vendors are much more aggressive, chasing us around. 'Hello … hello!'

The sales trick they use is to write the first price on their hands, then give you the pen and invite you to write your offer. One woman has an armful of truly ugly cushion covers—garishly machine-embroidered with crude hand stitching in the centre. The initial asking price is 80 yuan, which finally, after she has chased us to the bus, becomes 20 yuan.

The problem is I don't just dislike them. I hate them. She is the first of a long and noble line of salespeople that I am to meet in China who

筷子

simply can't understand that there will NEVER be a point where the price is low enough for their goods to suddenly become desirable. For them cheap is the only deciding factor. How can someone NOT like a thing if it is crazily underpriced?

This can be a limiting factor if you just like to browse. I argue that shopping for women is more about picking things up and turning them over, then putting them down again. Actually opening the purse and handing over money or your credit card in exchange for goods is a relatively infrequent action. This explanation sometimes helps to put colour back in the cheeks of men who have become pale and paralysed when their partner cheerily mentions that she is about to take off for 'a spot of retail therapy'. Guys, it's not going to cost too much. Trust me. I'm a woman, and that's how we (most of us) shop.

In many parts of Asia, and especially China, where capitalism is enjoying a well-deserved renaissance, marketing is a major industry. What's more, it seems that the shopkeepers, stallholders and anyone who operates any sort of commercial activity, from a mat on the footpath to a mega-store, are all acutely tuned in to not just body language, but any potential customer's line-of-sight.

Forget following up on anything you might inadvertently handle. By Day Two in China, only the reckless do that. Just to look at a scarlet snow dome, a nodding plastic beetle in a box, or a paper fan is enough for that object to be instantly picked up by the proprietor or salesperson (even if they are only four years old), and be demonstrated, praised and angled to show off its best advantage, along with a firm attempt to get you to take such a priceless bargain into your own hand to see for yourself at close range its finer points.

No need to haggle, either. A step forward on your journey, and the pitch continues. 'I give you very good price. How much you want to pay?'

Shaking your head is no disincentive. It translates as: 'obviously I don't want to pay so much. Okay, let's talk about the price.'

'How much? How much you want?'

Now remember, you haven't even looked at the object again. It is, after all, incredibly cheap and nasty. You only glanced at it in the first place because you couldn't believe your eyes. But now—according to your new bargaining partner—you want it, and you want it bad. In his or her mind, this is the sale of the day. The game is on, and who knows how low the price can go.

There are few rules in all this, but to successfully avoid most of this unwanted interaction you need to walk briskly through any market or shopping area with your eyes fixed directly ahead and TOUCH NOTH-ING, which—as any woman can tell you—is not really shopping.

If you can persevere, there are wonderful experiences to be had and lovely things that will—eventually—be perfect souvenirs. Yet, some things do not travel very well. At Kashgar, in what I call the 'Perth of China' because of its position on the far western border of this huge country, we spend a morning at a stock market. There are no bonds and shares here though. This is where the local farmers come to trade their sheep and goats, cattle, horses, donkeys and even camels, and I don't think I have ever enjoyed anything as much as our time here which segues on to the regular Sunday markets in the town itself.

筷子

We arrive early at the market grounds on the outskirts of Kashgar, or Kashi as it is sometimes called. This ancient city was one of the key Silk Road stopping points, a trading centre for centuries. Marco Polo commented on the fine gardens, orchards and vineyards he saw. Although Islam is alive and well here, Kashi was apparently one of the first Buddhist kingdoms in the area.

It is great to feel invisible when travelling, and while our pale Anglo-Celtic faces are totally different to the swarthy Turkic ones of the local Uigyar (pronounced wee-gwar) people, everyone is far too busy with the business of selling off their stock to care about us at all. The men, wearing elderly navy or grey suits and cloth caps, the women in head scarves and long patterned skirts, cluster around the animal pens. Occasionally we have to skip aside as an ancient red or blue truck piled high with bags of cotton, children, black or brown or white goats and sheep, honks at us to move, or a wooden cart rumbles against our heels. Soon we are covered in dust and the acrid smell of animal droppings. But so is everyone else.

To one side a long line of booths is empty. 'It's Ramadan,' our guide tells us, 'usually these are filled by people selling food.'

I am disappointed; I'd wanted to see what the locals would have bought to eat on the run as they haggle and bargain. Just one or two places hold mounds of golden breads shaped like bagels. While most of the vendors aren't eating, they are buying carcasses of freshly killed meat from gory lines hung above some stands. These will go home with them to be cooked for much awaited after-sunset feasts when they may eat after fasting all day.

The animals are segregated by species. At one point we find a donkey tied securely to a crude timber stand. We are glad to learn that this is not some cruel Kashgarian punishment, but simply a way to keep him still while he has his shoes changed. A man in one of those square embroidered caps, traditional in this area, sits on the ground nearby beating an iron crescent into shape on a well-worn anvil. He is surrounded by a mound of horse—or in this case donkey—shoes and stout nails, so it seems he is looking at a busy day ahead.

I later buy one of those stiff caps, mainly because I like the lady who is selling them, and especially when she shows me the major selling point—it can fold absolutely flat for packing. I can always be won over by a sales-pitch like that or some nifty little extra pocket, especially if it is cunningly concealed.

At the gate to the main sales ring, we pass stands selling leather belts, reins and harnesses that have the local farmers very interested. One man sits beside a heap of halters contrived from old car tyres, which have been bent to an oval then tied firmly and finished with a natty red wool tassel that sits up dandily above the horse's shoulders.

We see plenty more of these later when we visit the bustling markets in the town. There, dressed in their best, entire families cram onto their donkey-drawn drays, and pack the narrow streets. Without much room to move, as the footpaths are equally full of vendors, the scene morphs into some sort of a slow motion folk dance—a ballet from another age—with donkeys in the cast.

We pass a young man in a white skullcap brandishing a sharp knife. He beckons to us, keen for us to notice his shining, chrome, cross-shaped machine—part Middle Ages torture instrument with sharp points and a hefty screw, part useful tool—and the rich crimson liquid bleeding into a red bucket below it. He has bottles of the stuff already filled, and just as we are about to shudder and turn away, we realise he is squashing the ruby juice from pomegranates. There are baskets of these pink globes everywhere, their skins split to reveal the glistening gem-like seeds. In the afternoon sun, they could have been still-life subjects for a Dutch-school painter.

Nearby, in a stand, shielded from the sun by multicoloured canvas, a man with a lovingly tended white beard carefully hacks slices from a sort of almond and walnut confectionery with a hunk of steel almost as big as

筷子

an axe-head. I would have liked to try some, but the equally interested crowd of flies got in the way.

Further along, we see immense slabs of plain cake sitting in the sun. Beside them a boy fills a plastic bag, fashioned to create a disposable icing bag, from a tub of frosting and squirts it onto cakes to order. The customers then take away their chunk of freshly iced cake in a polystyrene container, feeling very satisfied, I'm sure.

Other stalls sell noodles and stir-fry dishes, and it seems that here at least is a Ramadan-free zone as plenty of snacking is going on. Then we round a corner and I am faced—literally—by one takeaway that I will not succumb to. A pile of roasted sheep's heads on a barrow eye me sleepily. They have apparently been boiled then roasted, entirely whole—lips, nostrils, eyes, horns, all quite visible—and are no doubt a huge local delicacy, but enough to make most Westerners flinch.

Luckily, right beside them, on the ground, something takes my mind entirely off those gruesome gourmet treats. Here, baskets and baskets of lush green figs lie shielded from the sun by giant fig leaves, and I know exactly how good these will be. This is a fig variety that I eat at home, and although the skin is a rather uninteresting greenish-yellow, once split open it reveals a pot of honey-gold flesh of melting sweetness.

I happily hand over a few yuan, and within a few paces of the stall scoff my treasures from their newspaper wrapper, peeling off the skin for safety's sake, even though I would love to consume them whole.

To me this is the whole point of shopping in a foreign country—finding treasure, often in unlikely places, and whether it will be for me or as a gift for friends at home, is not the point. It's the thrill of discovery. When you think about it, gifts are a way of achieving some sort of unintended immortality. People are loath to throw them out, especially if they have come from a far country, or from someone much loved. They tend to get passed around, and passed down. After all, how with a clear conscience and sane mind can you put that slab of slate painted with an alpine scene

筷子

that your grandmother lugged all the way home from Switzerland for you, out in the council cleanup?

On another trip, I spend a happy hour wandering the narrow laneways of a canal-side *hutong*, one of the few remaining villages of Beijing. Once there were thousands of these but Beijing's redevelopment has seen many residents move on to multi-storey apartments, and much of the city's land has been taken over by highways and factory sites.

Here, quaint stone houses wrap around serene courtyards locked off from the street by heavy doors. Some, however, allow a peep into another world, and as I pass by I get a glimpse of life going on as it always has.

Brilliant red-canopied pedicabs, trimmed with gold fringes and filled with Westerners, overtake me. They are pedalled by equally handsomely clad riders, nipping between bikes and pedestrians, swerving to avoid each other and scooting down the narrowest lanes with only centimetres to spare. Occasionally they hoot out a greeting to one another.

This *hutong* is a labyrinth of cloned alleys with identical doorways and gates. The name *hutong*, our guide, Jolly, says, comes from a Mongolian word, meaning 'a well', and it makes sense that these villages would have sprung up around a communal watering place. As we walk around, she points out how the width of the doorway and number of steps identify which houses once belonged to a nobleman or official and which did not.

We arrive in one of these at our bed and breakfast, as far as I know the only one in this city of twelve million—but more of that later—our luggage occupies another, as this is the only way to reach the innermost recesses of a *hutong*. Unless you walk.

The main shopping street seems relatively unaffected by tourism. In some shops, flat golden loaves of fried bread, cut through to show how they have been folded, are displayed temptingly at hand level; at others, fat steamed dumplings in bamboo baskets breathe mist into the morning air. Some, which I suspect are filled with red bean paste, have been dipped in sesame seeds and snipped at the edges like a chrysanthemum.

Because these *hutongs* are becoming trendy places to visit, there are occasionally cafés or places with bright cushions and lounges that I am told are pretty hip bars after dark. One advises 'Have a Appointment with Heaven, The Romantic Beer Bar of Tibet!'

Above another shopfront with a tiny sign proclaiming, 'coffee. t a. cake' I can just see a rooftop terrace with a few scraggly shrubs, some metal chairs and a couple of green umbrellas—no doubt supplied by the drink company 'Chill' whose matching sign and logo hangs below.

I resist the chopsticks and their rests nestled in gold silk-lined boxes, a fierce moustachioed puppet, even the option—taken up by many—of renting a bike and skimming along the footpath beside the canal. We are flying out today, and I am not quite sure what I am looking for, but when I round a corner, I know that this is where I should spend my few remaining yuan.

This is the Beijing equivalent of Caterer's Warehouse, and here are all the accoutrements coveted by any self-respecting Chinese restaurateur and chef. While the front part contains all the tools of the trade you would expect, the back is given over to massive woks and wok burners, huge gleaming stainless steel cauldrons and pots large enough to cook up a feed for the Red Army if necessary.

Even a confirmed shopaholic like me knows that to spend long in this section is folly—the overhead locker can only take so much—so I work my way back to the front of the shop, past the shelves and shelves of blue and white crockery, the massed bundles of chopsticks and heaps of ceramic pots and clay saucepans.

There I wonder at ladles as large as a basketball, and wire strainers of every size, cleavers and knives, and moulds to make the endless array of steamed cakes that the Chinese love so much. A tower of bamboo steamers totters above me, beside rolling pins of every width and length. Here is a truly wondrous array, slightly resembling a similar store back home—there are plenty of pans and implements I recognise—but perfectly Chinese at the same time.

筷子

Then I see what I have unconsciously been seeking all along. I'm a gadget gal and here is a dream come true. In a nifty black compendium, the size of a paperback, every tool you could ever need for carving, shaping, decorating and tooling food is carefully anchored in its place. Melon ballers, grooving tools, sharp things to fringe and slice and corrugate carrots and zucchini and ... oh, a thousand uses, I can see immediately.

Most amazing is the price, 24 yuan—around AUD$4. I know in a breath that I have to have it.

'Will you ever use it?' asks practical Gordon when I show it off, back at the B&B, before packing it deep in my suitcase. It will travel safely in the hold, and no awkward questions at the check-in either. No one is going to make me give up this prize.

'Of course I will!' I am amazed he could even ask such a question.

I will too—one day. For now it is safely in my pantry, the price still on it. After all, it would have been a crime to pass up such a bargain.

筷子

# 2. BEIJING: HEAVEN AND HUTONGS

*Force tells weak from strong for a moment; truth tells right from wrong all the time.*

**Chinese Proverb**

A kite swoops against the brilliant blue sky over Tiananmen Square. Its face has a dragon on it, of course, and I have seen them dozens of times already in Beijing. They are synonymous with China, the premier birth sign and a symbol of power and authority.

The Great Wall, north of the city, meanders over ridges like a giant dragon too, constructed to defend the southern regions and the precious silk route from the marauding hordes of Mongolia. Dragons are mythical beasts though and the threat from the north has long diminished. Silk is no longer the prized and precious creation it once was, unique to China, with its secret carefully guarded.

We have been in the capital only a couple of days, but already I can see that today's Beijing is steadfastly looking forward. While the past is its foundation, everywhere we see signs proclaiming 'Beijing 2008' and the hum of preparation is a reminder of Sydney's cleanup prior to the 2000 Olympic Games. Although they are still a couple of years away, you sense that China will be ready well ahead of schedule.

Although Beijing, the capital, with its necessary air of solid administration, is home to thirteen million people, it is not China's largest city. The mega-industrial city of Chongqing and look-at-me Shanghai each outsize it. Beijing's blocks of buildings are chunky and square, separated by long straight wide roads, many of them tree-lined, which softens the military layout. Chang'an Avenue (which translates as 'the avenue of everlasting peace') is 120 metres wide, the longest and widest city-centre street in the world, I am told.

Even the city's three million cars seem to move in a more orderly fashion, and that jostling jumble of bicycles that creates havoc in other cities is much smaller here. We see Passats and Citroens, Hondas, Jeeps and Santanas, and Flag cars which we don't recognise, but learn that they are made in Inner Mongolia. Giant Bicycles seem big here, and are advertised—along with their website—on a billboard.

We head off early on our first morning for Tiananmen Square, of course, the largest city square in the world. Our guide tells me that it is said that one million people can assemble here in the forty-plus hectares, the stark expanse of concrete paving stones softened by gardens and fountains.

Mao's portrait presides over a building on the far side. He looks almost benign so I weaken and buy a Mao wristwatch from a man with a tray of them who is working the tourists in the square. Mao waves in time with the seconds. Tick-wave, tick-wave. The round face seems friendly, and the waving hand gives a cheery salute. It stops keeping time the next day, needless to say—those cheap buys inevitably do—but Mao keeps waving.

A soldier stands guard in front of Mao's picture, immovable in his braided, peaked cap and khaki uniform with gold buttons flashing in the sunlight. We see the many faces of China pass by as we stand there. A student cycles along the road behind him; nearby a family group poses for a photograph, the tiniest child wriggling in impatience to be going;

筷子

an old lady in a shapeless grey coat hobbles past them; while a bunch of young people lounge around the base of a lamp post. Some are talking on their mobiles. One reads a newspaper.

A tiny child in a red tracksuit stands with his parents, unimpressed—or maybe overcome—by the crowds. He holds a small red and yellow paper flag with its five stars in his hand. The big star denotes Communist rule, the four smaller ones curled around it are for the fifty-six nationalities in China. The red stands for the blood of the soldiers.

While this is the modern face of Beijing—affable guards resigned to having their pictures snapped, tourists at every turn—an equally important movement is this return of open pride in China's heritage. So we head for a place that is now no longer out of bounds. The Forbidden City was the imperial residence for 600 years, kept secret from the eyes of commoners. Today it is called the Palace Museum, a tranquil and beautiful magnet for all.

We enter, not by the most-used gate, the South Gate, because it is under renovation, but by the Flowery Gate, once used by concubines. The Forbidden City has 9,999.5 rooms, says Jane, our guide. She has told us her Chinese name, but knows we will not remember it, or won't be able to pronounce it, so like most others she has adopted a Western name. 'The heavenly king has 10 0000 rooms, so nowhere on this earth may have as many.'

The highest building in Beijing is fifty-three storeys, Jane tells us. This is because the Forbidden City is in the centre, and the city must remain in scale. In fact the same city shape has been retained since the time of the grandson of Genghis Khan.

To the south stands the imposing Temple of Heaven. Its three round roofs over a square building depict the sky above the earth. This is where the Ming and Qing dynasty (1368–1911) emperors came to ask for the one thing they could not control, a good harvest. We walk around The Hall of Prayer for Good Harvests, built in 1420 and apparently meant for a different use. The sign outside says it was originally named 'The Great Hall for Sacrificial Rituals'.

I am glad that I have good walking shoes for Beijing. There is so much to see, and so many steps to climb. But, the following day Jane thinks we need a relaxing break and directs us to the Summer Palace, built around a lake in the northwest of the city. Here I get a feel for how the Empress Dowager Ci Xi in the late 1800s endured Beijing's steamy hot season. The palace is built around the K'unming Lake and we stroll on the lakefront, passing carved stone animals and vendors, with views of the palace rising pagoda-like above the water on the far side.

We cross the lake in a boat that looks like a summerhouse perched on a dragon's back. The roof is tiled like a mini-pagoda, the hull is moulded and painted with scales and the prow is a realistic head with glaring eyes and bared teeth. You'd think children would be frightened, but the boat is full of families seated on the wooden benches, and I remind myself that this is China and these kids have seen dragons all their lives.

We disembark just a few minutes later near the white, multi-arched and suitably Venetian-looking Marco Polo Bridge. It curves elegantly over the water and we walk across it with all the other tourists who pause to take pictures of each other.

Gordon, of course, takes pictures of them taking pictures of each other, the bridge, the lake and the palace in the distance or anything else that's interesting. He has always been prolific in his picture taking. I don't call him the Mad Photographer for nothing, but digital photography has given him endless freedom. Now he does not have to consider the cost of film and processing, he has become an even more ardent shutter-bugger.

At one point we see dozens of small pink and green fibreglass boats moored among waterlilies, waiting to propel couples out onto the lake for an afternoon of fun on the water. Nearby a woman in a headscarf and a blue dustcoat over jeans wields a straw broom, brushing away leaves from the paths.

筷子

The lake freezes over in winter, here in China's cold north-east. It is said that the Empress had her servants cut chunks of ice from its surface and store them in underground cellars where they remained until she needed chilled drinks the following summer.

It's not all history in Beijing. One morning we visit some black-eyed beauties at the Beijing Zoo. There, several lazy pandas stretch voluptuously on their log perches, sunning themselves, oblivious to their responsibility of keeping their species alive. Right now they are more interested in gnawing on a bunch of tender bamboo leaves and soaking up the attention from the crowds that stand in awe of them.

'Are they dangerous?' I ask with black bears and grizzlies in mind.

Jelly is our new guide, who has chosen a fun name instead of a traditional one.

'No,' she giggles. 'They are very gentle. They like to play.'

Then she says, 'I will tell you a joke. Do you know what is the biggest wish of a panda?'

Of course we don't.

'To take a colourful picture!' And she laughs in delight.

These are fun creatures, too. The cute eye patches and the large head, in relation to the body, add to the giant panda's stuffed-toy appearance. The Chinese call them by a phrase that translates as 'giant cat bear'. I look them up later and find that indeed they are bears, but maybe it's something in bamboo that contributes to their benign personalities.

They must really love those tender shoots because an adult panda will consume up to fifteen kilograms of bamboo branches, stems and leaves daily. It is said they can eat up to thirty-eight kilograms of these tasty morsels, which is around forty per cent of their average bodyweight. It is lucky for them that bamboo grows so quickly—up to a metre a day sometimes, or around five centimetres an hour! Otherwise they would soon run out of food in their natural habitat.

Another night we enter the realms of culture—Chinese tourist-style—with a trip to the Opera at the Liyuan Theatre. The lyrics are subtitled so we can grasp something of the storyline, but it hardly matters as the expressions on the heavily made-up faces and the wildly coloured costumes are almost entertaining enough by themselves. In fact when I do try to follow the tale, it is almost plotless—boy meets girl, boy catches girl. That's it.

No trip to Beijing would be complete without a dinner of Peking duck. Our meal, at a table pressed up right alongside the kitchen's window, one evening, allows us front-row viewing of theatre of another kind. We watch enthralled as chefs in immaculate whites swing out a convoy of gleaming tanned ducks, hanging them just above us, on the other side of the glass.

A starched and aproned waiter carves our portions table-side, then mimes the process of placing duck slices with onion and hoi sin sauce inside a wrapper selected from the large stack of pancakes provided in our own personal bamboo steamer. Patiently they tutor us in the best way to roll the pancake so that we don't squirt sauce and duck fat down our chests. It seems such a large stack of pancakes to begin with, but the crispy duck pieces are so delicious, and the combination of sweet and salty, crisp and smooth so delectable, we finish most of them.

筷子

Another evening we dine at the privileged China Club, set discreetly amongst trees in a quiet street. It's very genteel and we take drinks, seated in leather armchairs in the library, before moving on to the dining room in another building across the courtyard. If I didn't know otherwise, I could easily imagine this is someone's own luxurious home.

Ying, our host, is a member here, and we are suitably awed to be afforded this glimpse into another side of Beijing life, one which few tourists see. Yet, once seated at the round, polished timber table, the sequence of dishes arrive with the usual efficiency. We could be anywhere China.

A spicy soup, with fragments of egg and tiny cubes of tofu floating in the silken broth, arrives first. This is followed by suitably fiery Szechwan prawns and steamed buns that squeak as we bite into them and help put out the flames. Duck, of course, this time smoked, and served in a soy sauce, with rice, and a dessert of watermelon, orange and kiwi fruit, which reminds me of course that this latter fruit is a local, known here as a Chinese gooseberry.

Just one thing chills us that lovely evening. As we drive down one of Beijing's major boulevards we exclaim over a beautiful neon rainbow, unlike any I have seen. The multicoloured bands rise from each side of the road, but the centre remains incomplete.

'Why is it that way?' I ask.

'That side is for when Hong Kong came back,' says our driver, matter-of-factly, 'and the other side is for when Macau came back.'

'But what about the middle?' I persist.

'That is for when Taiwan comes back.'

We make a last trip to the hutong, to sip green tea with Mr Jing our host at the bed and breakfast. We sit overlooking the pomegranate tree in the centre of the space between the various wings of his home. His family has lived here for a century but now that he and his wife and son operate the home-stay programme, he hosts people from all over the world.

Insulated from the hubbub of this giant metropolis, I think about Beijing, an ancient city that has endured so much: wars, revolution, emperors and dissidents. There are temples imploring heaven for rain in the right season, and humble homes opening their doors to strangers.

Somehow Mr Jing's welcome seems a fitting metaphor.

*A soldier stands guard at Tian'anmen Square*

筷子

# 3. ALARUMS AND EXCURSIONS

*A gem is not polished without rubbing, nor a man perfected without trials.*

**Chinese Proverb**

I know we are in for a rough night when the tent blows down. Rather, it sort of collapses in on us, the metal poles that have created a crawl space at the doorway buckling under the force of the wind. I wake only moments before it happens, shaken out of my sleeping tablet induced euphoria by what sounds like sharp rain snapping on the nylon tent-fly centimetres above my head.

I calm myself. Hey, this must be what it was like in the old windjammers, the sails flapping and straining in the gale. Well, I am partly right. It is a blizzard. Within a moment, there is a flurry of panicky Tibetan being shouted through the tent zip. You don't have to be a linguist to work out that this means 'Get out! Fast'.

Damn. This was the first night I had looked like sleeping well in days. I am staying free of most of the effects of AMS (Acute Mountain Sickness) such as the headaches, nausea and diarrhoea that many of the other dozen or so members of our group are suffering, but I've been plagued by insomnia, another common complaint of travellers hitting the high altitudes.

That night my mattress had been flat as a tack. Something to do, I guess, with my decreased lungpower when blowing it up. I can tell you that in a contest between the ground-zero cold of the Tibetan Plateau and one Australian's body heat, the Aussie comes a poor second. I figure I am basically trying to warm up Tibet and, funnily enough, not succeeding. All those high school physics classes on how some things take latent heat out of other things suddenly make sense. Proving, I guess, you just can't beat cold hard facts.

Dragging on my boots, which I have luckily left parked neatly inside the door flap, I am so thankful that this is the first night on the trip I have chosen to go to bed fully clothed. Not premonition. I'd simply been too breathless and exhausted in the increasingly thin air to struggle with changing inside something the size of a doona cover.

We grab our belongings that have been scattered around our mats and stuff them into a tote bag, then stumble out into pitch darkness, snow flying horizontally past our startled noses. It is like being sucked into a spin dryer.

Nearby the Tibetan drivers are coming to grips with the emergency.

Jimmy—our man, the same one who each day coolly skitters our Land Cruiser centimetres from 1000-metre drops and negotiates landslides, blind corners and hairpin bends without a shudder—is babbling uncontrollably in Tibetan as he tries to convert what had been, until moments before, his bedroom into our escape vehicle. Now the 4WD suddenly assumes heroic proportions as we bundle inside.

The headlights bore holes in the snowy curtain and we watch the other members of our group, just as disoriented, scramble around, trying to locate their luggage in the dark. It is a shaky little convoy, then, that finally inches off the river flat that had looked so safe just hours before. The lights now glare on the snow-driven test pattern almost concealing the road leading to the town a few kilometres away. In itself, this is a miracle. We've had several nights on the road and, most times, have camped hours away from civilisation, unless you counted the nomads—shapeless in their heavy felt coats—who would materialise just as we set up camp.

Of course, if you took time to look, their black tents were always nearby, the smoke rising through the vented roof, a cluster of equally black yaks grazing in a crude stockade beside them. The children, like kids anywhere, would swarm silently around the perimeter of our activity or line up solemn-faced and amazed at the sight of us. Sometimes there would be a small girl with a baby strapped to her back, while others hauled bundles of sticks.

The women, with cheeks rouged to soreness by the bitter climate, carried their wealth—chunks of turquoise the exact colour of the rivers we occasionally dropped down to cross—sewn onto their clothes, woven into their long black plaited hair or mounted on rings. Sometimes they drew engraved silver daggers from within the folds of their clothing, not in any kind of anger—for these peaceful people were as fascinated by us (who knows, maybe more so) as we were by them—but to trade or sell. The yuan we paid would buy useful things: matches and blankets, food and needles.

As we roll into the muddy yard of the large hotel in Nagqu, north-eastern Tibet, it could be The Ritz, so grateful are we to be there. Indeed, finally having a room with a real bed and a real toilet, not to mention a shower, is luxury unimaginable. There are even disposable slippers, combs in little cardboard wrappers, and toothbrushes. Yet sleep eludes me as I lie rock-cold and shivering in the unfamiliarly soft bed, the adrenalin rush of the past couple of hours still at high tide.

Yup! Not one of the best nights I've ever had. But at least I know now that I can always quite truthfully answer when people ask me about my impressions of Tibet: 'Loved it. Loved the people, loved the scenery. Yes, it quite literally blew me away!'

In fact, we've already encountered a bit of action on this trip. Just days

筷子

earlier we had come to a full stop behind our supply truck which itself was trapped behind a local timber truck that had broken an axle and was occupying most of the narrow road between massive rocks on one side and a sheer drop on the other. The timber truck's occupants, mainly women and youngsters, had scrambled down from the tray and were spilling over the road. The men were already up-ended under the vehicle and looking at the damage, but it was the women, up close, that had me astounded. Their high cheekbones and skin scuffed raw made them look more South American than Tibetan. Even their clothes—flowing, densely woven garments, topped by a sort of an apron—didn't match the rest of China. The weight of the turquoise they carried, their currency, must have been substantial, but they wore it easily, and their quick, confident smiles made me wish I knew more than just *Tashi Delek* (good morning) so I could converse with them. They were making the best of it and had already set up a tent, prepared to camp out on the roadside until the road cleared. We had the feeling this was not such an unusual situation and used the hold-up as a chance to take photos and discuss the event with each other.

Then two more trucks came from the opposite direction loaded with monks—pilgrims from Lhasa—in maroon and gold robes. It was a regular traffic jam in an irregular setting, and we took plenty of photographs. I also fixed one young girl's sore finger with some Betadine and my fancy cartoon character Bandaids, brought all the way from Australia for just such an emergency.

At last faithful Jimmy was able to squeeze our 4WD through the narrow space beside the truck by folding in the rear-view mirrors. With many hand signs and beckoning, the rest of our convoy followed us. But there was no way our supply truck could get through.

Only a few kilometres further down the road our 4WDs became bogged too. Some days are like that. It's funny, isn't it? Usually the equipment you take with you is the right thing, but for the wrong occasion.

筷子

For example, I always begin to giggle when the flight attendant presenting the safety talk before take-off gets to the part about 'and your life vest has a light here and a whistle for attracting attention'. Now really, rather than a whistle, I would greatly prefer a can of shark repellent. Think about it: how unlucky would this be? Survive the crash and get trimmed by a shark or a crocodile. Even eaten alive by mosquitos in a tropical jungle sounds pretty unattractive, so maybe add some mozzie repellent too.

While we're at it, could we also have a small can of rations, please? Something to munch on while waiting to be rescued. Nothing too elaborate. A flask of something comforting (Jack Daniels would do) and some snacks from economy class. After all they are so dry to start with they should last several days.

It is a dark and stormy night—well dark, anyway—and we have arrived in Lijiang, also in south-western China, but don't read anything into this, please. It's a perfectly good part of China.

On this trip we are with a group of about twenty others on a bus with Tony, our Chinese guide, and have reached our hotel late in the afternoon. Like many Chinese hotels it is set back from the road and accessed through wide, pillared gates. The foyer, like so many others, is a welcoming riot of gold and red and shiny surfaces.

As is often the case we have barely time to put our cases down before heading out for dinner. That's the way of tour groups, and the Chinese. Eat early, eat quickly, go home, go to bed. So we set off for the restaurant a few blocks away, talking and stumbling on the rough footpaths. My sense of direction is non-existent so I keep with the others. I am not sure how tour groups are selected. It can't be at random as they seem to conform to a very strict template. There is always one know-it-all who corrects the guide. There are the ones who snooze the entire time, making you wonder why they bothered to come at all. Then there are those who are perpetually late, the ones the group hisses at as they finally, finally climb the steps into the coach or emerge from the lift into the lobby for dinner, fifteen minutes over-time.

My friend Amy told us on her return from a coach tour in Scotland, that she'd been enjoying herself just fine. Got off the coach at some heathery little cuppa-tea stop and got back on again with everybody else. Twenty minutes and a short doze later, she took stock of her companions and recognised none of them. It took her two days and dozens of phone calls to get back with her own group. She had re-routed herself to Inverness, while they were still enjoying the Borders.

Ours of course has representatives of all of these sub-groups, plus an eccentric academic or two, a man from another planet, Brian (we'll come to him) and two perfectly normal human beings, just for balance. The latter being us, you realise.

Brian moves in a sort of fog. He is an older man and a serial tourist, but that isn't all. He is somehow detached. 'I've got another big trip coming up next year,' he tells us one day, 'but I can't remember where it is. It's on a train, somewhere.'

After dinner, as we start to walk back to the hotel, the group separates into two, quite naturally, as groups do. I am amongst the loiterers bringing up the rear when Tony starts to panic. Chinese are renowned for keeping a calm face, but he is visibly worried.

筷子

'Where's Brian?' he cries out. 'Anyone seen Brian?'

We haven't, and the other group hasn't, Tony reports when he gets back to where I have waited on a corner. My companions have gone on by now. It's pitch dark, few streetlights and me with just the dimmest recollection of where exactly we are.

'I have to go look for him,' says Tony, who frankly has no idea in the world where to start in a city of this size. 'Can you find your own way back to the hotel?'

Me? ME???

'Yes, sure, no problems.' After all, I'm a travel writer, aren't I?

Now, you have to remember that I had taken very little notice of how we had arrived at the restaurant. My biggest problem is that my attention gets diverted by transient attractions—dogs, people, cats, bicycles— things that won't necessarily still be there when I want to use them as a landmark at a later time.

I can vaguely remember the gateway for the hotel, and the cavernous black courtyard beyond. But—and here is the crucial mistake—I have come away from it without the hotel business card with its name written in Chinese. I am not too sure whether I even remember its name in English.

Which is how it happens that within minutes I am lost, alone, on a dark street in a city in south-western China—which we have already affirmed is a very fine part of the country—so I am not afraid for my personal safety, as such. That's if you don't count breaking a leg in the dark on the catastrophic footpath, or catapulting down an open manhole. I do want to see my bed tonight and I can't help but notice the irony of the guide looking for one tour member, while another one gets lost.

So I do what anyone else would do in such a situation—I panic! No, I don't really. I do the perfectly sensible thing and what anyone else would do (here in Australia, anyway) and go into a shop to ask directions. It sells watches and the two people behind the counter couldn't be more

筷子

helpful—or more devoid of English or (in my opinion) intelligence, at that moment.

I mean how can you not understand a slightly deranged Australian woman saying 'Hotel' very clearly, in English while bending her head sideways onto her folded hands and closing her eyes? I feel it is a very fair impression of a person wishing to fall asleep. After all isn't that the prime use of hotels? On second thoughts, I guess I could use other words and actions, but that might have me locked up or being the focus of another—and unwanted—sort of attention.

Of course there is nil comprehension of my pantomime, replayed several times in the various small shops that are still open along that road. By this time I have lost all sense of just how far we walked down this road before dinner. I don't know whether I have gone too far or not far enough. Just as hysteria is about to kick in, I come across a vaguely familiar pair of pillared gates and realise, with a rush of relief, that this is my hotel. A garish, shiny lobby has never looked so good.

And Brian? Tony tells us, the next morning at breakfast, that he found Brian in another hotel nearby ... sitting in an identical, shiny red and gold lobby waiting for us all to catch up or something.

*The winding streets of Li Jiang*

# 4. DUMPLING DAYS

*Teachers open the door. You enter by yourself.*

**Chinese Proverb**

Mrs Jing is giggling at me. She doesn't speak English, but the message is clear. My dough and rolling pin technique is, quite clearly, hilarious. She has already demonstrated what I must do to help her make dumplings for the family dinner. Pinch off an egg-sized piece of dough, roll it into a ball then roll it out thinly. Hers turn out as perfect rounds. Mine resemble a map of Australia or, more possibly, China.

Right now I am a very temporary resident of Beijing: one night only, staying in the Jings' spare bedroom, one of three available to paying guests at their B&B. Once the idea of B&B's catches on, it will be a hit, I'm sure. The family welcomes groups who, as part of a pedicab tour of the hutong, visit briefly for a cup of green tea, chat and a nosey into the family's quarters. It's a fun way to see the area and the drivers clearly enjoy their role—swooping around the narrow lanes with their charges and exchanging good-natured banter with other riders. It's heavy work sometimes. Even though the distances are not great, Beijing can be steamy and hot.

Many of these village houses were built in the Ming and Qing dynasties, although some are more recent. From deep within there are all the usual suburban sounds—a television blares, there's the chirrup of a phone, and babies demand attention.

The Jings' gate has a secure iron grille and a lock, but inside a moon gate frames the courtyard with its ancient pomegranate tree. Several generations of the family have lived here in the past 100 years yet the home remains unpretentious and authentic, like so many others in this hutong.

*A moon gate frames the Jing's courtyard*

Our room is squeaky clean and simple: two single beds under pretty patterned coverlets, a few hooks for our clothes and a table. There's a heater, too, but we don't need it in October. There are two pairs of slip-on sandals for when we cross the courtyard at night to use the family bathroom in another wing. The other two guest bedrooms share a second bathroom.

Disconcertingly the family's dog, a large and lively collie, is named Shally (maybe Sha Li, who knows?) but it sounds close enough to my name to have the couple in fits of giggles once they recognise the resemblance.

My pastry rolling aside, the dumpling preparation is pretty straightforward. Once I have achieved something resembling a circle, I add a dab of filling (pork mince and herbs, already prepared by Mrs Jing) before folding the circles into half moons. Then comes the tricky bit, so she demonstrates it. Pleat the edges to seal in the filling, more so at the corners so they become a vague crescent shape.

I try to follow her swift, experienced moves to create something like the demo model. At least she doesn't giggle again. Mr Jing is kind enough to tell me it is very good.

Fortunately a hundred or so (it seems) of these later, I am off duty, able to relax until the call to dinner, a simple family meal at the family table. We are the only guests tonight, but son, Jimmy, is here and so is a boarder, a student from Korea.

Everyone else, naturally, is more adept with chopsticks than we are, but we manage the dunk-and-heat routine of the hot pot. The Jings use an electric version, bubbling and full of stock. We talk and share stories as best we can as we dip wafer thin beef slices, vegetables and steamed dumplings (I recognise some as my handiwork) into the savoury broth.

I want to stop the clock to make this evening, wrapped in the Jings' warmth and hospitality, last longer. To feel the heartbeat of a home, which places any tourist meal in a restaurant or any glittering cultural dance performance—even those complete with tumblers and acrobats—in perspective.

Midday, the following day, after a leisurely stroll around the local shops—taking care not to become disoriented by the baffling sameness of the laneways—we return to say goodbye to our hosts. Mrs Jing emerges from the kitchen, wiping her hands. Her husband explains that she's making dumplings for a group of ten people due anytime soon for lunch. I can't help noticing—with some surprise—that she hasn't called on my newly gained and, I feel, formidable dumpling-shaping skills. Maybe next time.

Some days before this, in Tianshui, I was given another dumpling lesson, with a difference. Here, our hotel window overlooks an apartment block and—with some time to spare late on a grey and drizzly morning—I take up the irresistible pastime of sticky-beaking across the laneway.

Many of the windows are empty. No doubt many people, as in Australia, are at work during the day, but some are occupied making lunch. Most of these seem to be boiling up vats of noodles.

One kitchen window, directly opposite, catches my eye, however. Here a woman is busying herself with a big bowl of flour and a long rolling pin. Behind her she has a pot of water coming to the boil and I watch mesmerised as she first mixes flour and water to a smooth dough, then rolls and re-rolls her dough on a whopping board until it becomes a huge sheet. This she sprinkles with salt and cuts into long strips about ten centimetres wide, dusting them with flour, stacking them two on two, before meticulously slicing them into triangles. She is really slow in her movements—painstakingly so—and I am just glad she isn't working for me, paid at an hourly rate.

By now she has noticed my interest and we exchange little waves. Mine saying, 'Do you mind?' Hers telling me that she is okay about my snooping, but she doesn't play up to the extra-curricular interest at all and simply keeps on working.

I can't see all her moves, but after a while—when everything is to her liking, no hurry—this is the task of her day, obviously, though whether it is for her family or for an order from a nearby restaurant I'll never know—she separates the triangles and begins to fill them with what I presume is something savoury.

Methodically, she tops each small piece of dough with a tiny dab of filling, twisting the corners to meet and seal it in. Thousands of kilome-

筷子

tres away, I realise, an Italian housewife could be doing much the same and serving her dish up to her family as tortellini.

By the time she has her floured board crammed with many dozens of these morsels, the pot of water is bubbling and she turns away into the steam, tumbling them in. If I could find a way across, I would run down to see for myself how long it takes them to cook and what she has been stuffing them with ... and what they taste like, of course.

Then from somewhere ('this is one I prepared earlier') she brings out more dough which she cuts into small knobs, rolling each to a wafer-thin circle, this time brushing them with oil. Chilli or sesame, I wonder? Of course, I can't tell from here. She looks up and smiles at me, conscious that she is giving me an additional tutorial.

For these, she reaches into another dish, and smears a filling across half of each circle, before carefully folding them into half-moon shapes and pinching the edges slowly, carefully. A swift lick of glaze on top then these too are put to rest on a baking tray. It is obvious that they are not destined for the water. It's the oven or deep fryer for them.

Then the doorbell rings. The porters are outside waiting for the luggage. What bad timing! It's check-out time just as I am about to discover the next dish my new friend has in store. I wave, but she is head down concentrating on those dumplings and doesn't see me go.

筷子

## 5. HOW NOW MACAU? and other changes in China

*The person who removes a mountain begins by carrying away small stones.*

**Chinese proverb**

Custard. That's it!

I am seated on a bench surrounded by the absolutely irresistible, sweet smell of something rich and eggy. It doesn't take long to identify what it is, of course, for this is Macau and someone, is whipping up a batch of those delicious Portuguese custard tarts with the blistered brown tops. The ones that took me about thirty seconds to fall in love with.

Actually it didn't take me much longer to fall for Macau either. This place, called the 'waterlily peninsula' by the Chinese, was annexed by the Portuguese in the mid-sixteenth century, becoming Asia's business hub until Hong Kong came on the scene. It has remained war free for almost five centuries, if you don't count an attempted Dutch invasion in 1622. In 1999, also peacefully, Macau was handed back to China and today it operates as a Special Autonomous Region (SAR).

So how is life going here, since the handover? I ask a local resident: 'How is Macau, now?'

筷子

I am faintly amused at the elocution lesson sound of the question.

'Tourism is way up,' he tells me. Adding that Macau is an international microcosm of around 450 000 French, Belgian, German, Irish, English and Australian residents happily muddled into the Chinese, Portuguese and Macanese population. So why wouldn't a tourist from just about anywhere feel at home?

I make the trip to Coloane, a snoozy village south of the main city, on an island, joined by a causeway to another island, Taipa, and make a sweet detour. Lord Stow (aka Andrew Stow, no title just a BSc) is a British pharmacist who became fascinated by those heavenly flaky-and-creamy tarts on a visit to Portugal and decided he would master the recipe. Then, in a classic coals-to-Newcastle move, he began marketing them to this Portuguese outpost in Asia.

He set up Lord Stow's Bakery in a tree-shaded square, selling these pastries to the locals, along with a range of sandwiches and filled rolls. The tarts were no problem—in fact many say they are the best they have ever eaten and I agree—but to begin with Lord S's customers were not too sure about some of the other offerings, such as those oh-so-British sandwiches.

The day I visit, a hand-lettered sign offers 'Half Price Introduction' prices to sausage and tomato sandwiches, so that uncertain diners may have an inexpensive taste of this strange and exotic snack.

I buy a tart of course, because at home or here I just can't resist them. I eat it sitting on a pink seat outside and yes, it is good, even outdoing the one from the bakery at my hotel which I have—perhaps a little prematurely—set as my benchmark. Lord Stow's tart has just the right degree of wafer-meets-toffee to hang together as I bite through the soft filling. The custard itself is sweet enough to hold my interest, but not cloying. There is a hint of lemon that bounces through and—can it be—a dusting of cinnamon on top?

I move on to another cafe in the pretty cream and white colonnaded

筷子

main square to pump some newfound acquaintances for information about the new Macau. We chat over tall glasses of chilled fresh water-melon juice while it seems the rest of the island is enjoying a post-lunch nap.

Crime is down now, I am assured, since the handover and some of the crime gangs have been broken. Then they tell me an amusing tale. One of the Mr Bigs, a Triad gangster known as Broken Tooth, whose people had terrorised the population, has finally been captured, tried and put away ... for good. So crucial was his permanent detention that the government built his own personal gaol—just big enough for him, his cronies and his gaolers. My friends point it out to me as we drive back the few kilometres to the city.

In the main city of Macau the air is more businesslike. There is a colony of big international hotel chains, shops open late, no European-style siesta and every second person seems to be on a mobile phone.

In the main Senate Square, paved with those distinctive, swirling, wavelike tile patterns, throngs of tourists pose for a trad-Macanese shot, against a backdrop of the primrose-arched facades on the public build-ings. I meet my guide, Teresa.

'Hurry, we must be quick,' she greets me, in excellent English, 'we have so much to see.'

I realise just how much as she propels me on a whirlwind tour of: first the Guia Lighthouse, the oldest lighthouse on the Chinese coast, built in 1865, then through the avant-garde Museum of Macau and on to the nearby Monte Fortress with the same cannons that repulsed the Dutch.

Finally, out of breath and time, she leaves me beside the imposing, grey seventeenth-century facade of St Paul's church to wander back down to the main square at my own pace. As I do I pass shops selling everything from Chinese back-scratchers to balls of twine, boutiques crammed with size six dresses the size of a handkerchief and darkly aromatic shops full of herbal remedies.

筷
子

Crowning all else in the city is the Macau Tower, a soaring 338-metre high structure five minutes from the ferry terminal. Here you can shop, spin (in the 360-degree cafe) or skywalk the tower's exterior. The latter even more hair-raising if you take the 'X' option, minus the handrail and 233 metres above the ground. This place is not for the vertigo-prone, for even the observation lounge allows an unobstructed stomach-lurching view of the streets below.

I decide to pass on that and head towards the water which is never far away. I visit the Ecumenical Centre and am touched by this tribute to all faiths, topped by the controversial twenty-metre bronze Kun Iam Statue, poised like some gleaming Hindu Madonna on the water's edge. Bypassing the exhibits I take time to sit outside and soak in the view of the twin, silken serpentine bridges that link the island of Taipa to Macau city, (strictly speaking Macau is both the city and the entire region, which means that Taipa is also in Macau) before I head off for the Jetfoil to make a one-hour trip, returning to Hong Kong.

It's been a quick visit, but Macau is delighted with the thousands of visitors who flip across here for a few days or even hours. I've come at the wrong time for the fast cars in the Grand Prix season and I took a raincheck on those 'out there' adventures, but I loved the fusion food born of the various cultures that have shaped the place. One thing is very sure, I'll certainly miss those custard tarts.

While Macau's Portuguese background is just one example of China's multicultural heritage, Hong Kong too has been through some changes. Another trip, another time and I am sitting in the tour minibus ... at the lights, waiting. There's nothing else to do so I start counting. Ten, twelve, fifteen, twenty-one of the people that I can see nearby are doing it. The lights turn green and off we speed, leaving the boys and girls of that particular Hong Kong street corner still talking on their mobiles.

It's a city of mobile phones, actually. Our guide admits, 'I don't have a phone at home,' and gives that embarrassed little laugh some Chinese people do. 'I just give everyone my cell phone number.' As if on cue it rings or rather clatters out a tinny Asian pop song as it has done repeatedly all morning. Welcome to Communist China, or more specifically an SAR of the People's Republic of China, known to some as Hong Kong.

If you are wondering how this place is doing since the hand-over, the answer is pretty nicely thank you. Capitalism appears to be alive and well. The shopping centres are busy. A trendy new area pops up every now and again, complete with bars and Western-sleek restaurants. And communication is the name of the game.

A year or so after the handover, a mobile phone cost HK$150 but for that, I am told, you received 2000 minutes free. I do some quick calculations. In a population of almost seven million, if every second—or even third—person had a mobile phone and they make just one call an hour, that's one hell of a lot of microwaves zinging around at any one time.

Yet this is a city of opposites. One morning in tranquil Hong Kong Park far below the towering mirrored skyscrapers, I join a tai chi class before breakfast. It's a pathetic sight. I am one of ten uncoordinated Westerners trying to be 'alighting cranes', 'pouncing tigers' and 'elongating elephants' or whatever they call those moves. We end up with a new respect for the elderly citizens that turn out at dawn all over the country for their early morning callisthenics. Even though the moves are done at the speed of a slowed down movie, we find ourselves sweating with the exertion as our rigid legs and unsupple spines protest.

Our retirement-age, pyjama-clad instructor weaves amongst us, perilously close to having some 100-kilogram person topple onto him. He adjusts our arms telling us to point our toes outwards, to lift our chins or rotate our hips, before returning to 'assume the position' effortlessly in front of our group. A snapshot I took (well it was a weak excuse to stop standing on one leg for a while) shows us in a multitude of interpretations of his demonstration. No doubt he wrote us all off as hopeless.

筷子

I follow this experience with a visit to the Chi Lin Nunnery at Diamond Hill, Kowloon, redeveloped in recent times, yet built using an ancient method of wooden tenons instead of nails. At its entrance near the lotus pond, our guide delivers a lengthy lecture on the benefits of feng shui. In fact this belief is central it seems to architecture in this city.

'See this building,' our guide stops us outside a skyscraper. 'It went broke because the feng shui is all wrong. Look at the water feature. It is flowing out of the building. Everyone knows that it will never make money. All the profits must flow straight out!'

Later that day at Wong Tai Sin Temple, I pick up a sheet of paper with instructions for fortune telling using a bamboo container and numbered sticks. It directs me to the Fortune Telling and Oblation Arcade behind the temple, where small booths house serious gentlemen at the ready to read my palm or plot my future course.

While all this may seem archaic in a city that glows at night from the millions of flickering neon tubes and fairy-lit skyscrapers, beneath it all this is still a very Chinese place. I find myself remembering the words of Deng Xiaoping: 'In fifty years, China will be like Hong Kong.' For now, Hong Kong is also like China.

If his prediction comes true the rest of China will be laughing, HK is already booming. Our guide points out a passing Rolls Royce (HK has the highest per capita ownership of these cars). It's white with gold curtains.

'See that?' He's positively chattering with excitement. 'Look at the numberplate.'

I do, but it blurs into a mass of sixes and eights.

'That is very propitious. The number plate costs HK$7 million.' He laughs out loud. 'The car only costs HK$1.7 million.'

Yet not everyone is happy. Just a couple of years ago a thirty-year-old Brit, Matt Pearce, put on a horse costume and did a lap around a public racetrack. He was convicted of disorderly conduct and creating a public nuisance. He may not have attracted so much notice if he had not been

筷子

doing it to urge full democracy in China. It's not the first time either. In 1997 he dressed as Spider-Man and climbed a massive outdoor television screen, also as a pro-democracy stunt.

Over yum cha—lotus pastries and steamed buns served in pink bowls—in the heavily carved timber interior of the Luk Yu Tea House, which hasn't changed in decades, I am told that Hong Kong has the world's highest per capita ratio of restaurants and cafes (one for every 700 people, if you must know). I learn too that on Hong Kong Island a massively long, twenty-four storey escalator skims 210 000 workers daily from the bottom to the top of the business district in the morning and back again in the evening.

If stats are your thing the newish Hong Kong International Airport annually processes around thirty million-plus passengers—not counting those simply transiting—while the 83.7-kilometre Mass Transit Railway (MTR) deals with 2.4 million commuters daily and the AUD90-cent Star Ferry crossing of Victoria Harbour remains maybe the best value sightseeing trip in the world.

Although modern and ambitious, (HK has Asia's tallest observation tower, the world's largest neon advertising sign and the world's highest ratio of land conserved in country parks) you can still find men in Hong Kong with bamboo cages taking their singing birds for walks in a park. You have to like a place like that.

One night I dine with some friends at the Yung Kee Restaurant, now a magnet for well-heeled gourmets, which began sixty years ago when Mr Kam Shui Fai began serving roast goose from a food stall near the Hong Kong-Macau ferry terminal. That wonderful, fatty, savoury smell drew in everyone from the ferry crewmembers to tourists. Before he knew where he was he had a devoted following.

It's a classic poor-boy-makes-good story and as we walk into the marble foyer we bet the feng shui is fine here. This place has been ranked amongst the top restaurants in the world for decades and is heaped with

筷子

awards and medals every year, yet the restaurant seems proud of its roots. Hanging in a window there is still the food-stall sight of deeply tanned, roast geese, gently drizzling juices into plates below.

Our meal features roast goose, as it must. The bird is paired with a superb liver sausage and this alone would have been enough, but there is also a cloudy, yellow sea whelk soup, the fishy-tasting pieces curled up in the broth, and 'cloudy tea' smoked pork, the densely fatty skin a test for whatever diet we thought we were on. The menu tells me that we ate two other appetisers and six other courses that night, but all I can say is that roast goose must be a memory suppressant because at some point the details of the meal blur into a multitude of tastes and textures.

There is seemingly no easy way to explain this once-British, now-Chinese city either. No way to fast track to an understanding of it. Full of contradictions and sometimes an enigma even to those who know it best, Hong Kong is quite simply an intriguing and complex Chinese puzzle.

On yet another visit to China, outside a McDonalds I am accosted by two young Chinese girls with arms linked. Their confidence boosted by each other, they stand in front of me.

'Where are you from?' they ask me carefully, in school lesson format. 'You like Shanghai?'

Like so many others they are language students, eager to test their schoolroom phrases. We chat, they giggle and then they shyly offer, 'You look ex-otic.'

I have to make sure I've heard right, so I make them repeat it. This is a first, a compliment not generally associated with me. They're happy to say it over, enunciating each syllable and I can see they're for real. Apparently, blonde-red hair—curly too—is a rarity in the straight black-bobbed world they inhabit. I am delighted, hugely amused and hug this to myself as I relish telling all my friends about it later. Somehow, they don't seem as thrilled. Amazed, yes, and I think I hear a snide chortle or two. Oh, well.

Yet, hair—styles and colour—is one of the few things not on the

筷子

move in modern Shanghai, located midway on China's eastern coast, ten kilometres from the mouth of the Yangtze River. The cityscape—most of it constructed in the past decade—seems straight off a futuristic sketch pad.

Parts of it—especially when seen from the freeways and swooping flyovers—belong to what I tag as the 'ballpoint pen' school of architecture, on account of the many slender buildings, tall and cylindrical, with a conical top and pointed tip. Others look like they could have come straight from the set of Star Wars, their bobbles and flying-saucer shapes glowing pink and silver, frosty blue and amber and linked by impossibly thin towers.

We pass clean, bright and neat apartment blocks, but our guide mutters, 'See the seven-storey ones. They have no lift. Everyone wants a ten-storey one ... with a lift, then you don't have to leave your bicycle in the basement.'

From the rock-solid Bund—for a century or so everybody's favourite promenade spot—and backed by staid, bank-solid colonial buildings, the buildings on the other side of the sedate Huangpu River glow in a Manhattan-like clump. On the left, the Shanghai International Convention Centre, flanked by twin globes, complements the avant-garde Orient Pearl television tower behind. At 468 metres it is the tallest of its kind in

筷子

Asia and third tallest in the world. Behind them again the magic silver-wire structure of the 88-storey Grand Hyatt thrusts skyward.

It is hard to imagine that this city donated a word to our language—'shanghai'—because of the bars furnished with pretty girls who once lured men in to be abducted and put to use as coolie slaves.

Late one evening we take a little train—a funfair-meets-space-age creation—that dives under the river from the Bund through a tunnel blazing with psychedelic neon hoops, lights and fairy spangles. When we emerge, less than five minutes later, the incandescent glow of the Grand Hyatt still seems distant, but beckons us the last few blocks like some glowing mirage.

Finally there we take the whisper-soft lift to the fifty-fourth floor. Even at this elevation find we are merely in the lobby and must cross a shimmering marble expanse to take the second lift to the eighty-fifth floor before changing for yet another that transports us, quite literally, to Cloud Nine, the hotel's darkly atmospheric bar overlooking the sparkling sprawl that is Shanghai by night.

From here we can see it all: the river looping through the city, the areas that once housed opium dens, French colonial quarters, stately British mansions and homes of Chinese merchants. It was of this cosmo-politan and raunchy city that a missionary once said: 'If God lets Shanghai endure, he owes an apology to Sodom and Gomorrah.' You could see why someone once called it 'the city par excellence of two things, money and the fear of losing it'.

Today's Shanghai is buzzing, already regarded as the financial capital of China and some predict that it will one day dominate the world. With a population of almost 14 million it has the formula, you would imagine, for shocking traffic snarls, pollution and poverty, but Shanghai's public face is smiling.

'Look for the private cars,' our guide encourages us. 'See, there are none. Nobody drives here.'

It's true. Buses, motor scooters and taxis stream along the multi-laned, multi-level freeways in an orderly mass and the rare private vehicles are noteworthy. I ask a city entrepreneur if he drives in Shanghai. He has lived here for decades after all, but he grimaces and shrugs.

'I use a taxi,' he answers dismissively and later, when I take a half-hour cab ride across town for under AUD$10, I can see why.

The driver deposits me in bustling Nanjing Road, Shanghai's acknowledged shopping street. A few blocks up from the well-known Peace Hotel a wide pedestrian precinct, flanked by several department stores, offers limited safety as bikes and motor scooters are not prohibited and I need to be alert, ready to jump out of their way in a moment.

In one store a rousing march is playing when I enter and, under an extravagance of bulbous red Chinese silk lanterns hanging from the distant ceiling, the central fountain pulses in time to the music, coloured lights accenting the stanzas. Crowds of young Shanghainese, obviously with money to spend, push past me. A young Western woman nearby is being badgered by several Chinese beauty consultants to have her face made up and above me the atrium stretches six, seven floors maybe, heavy with carefully displayed, tantalisingly available merchandise.

This is the twenty-first century version of Communist China. Capitalism is obviously thriving here too. Upstairs I wander into teeny-bopper land and join the young face of China as they check labels and prices. Cashed up it seems. American, Italian and German labels swing from the garments in candy pink and baby blue, but I know that many are made in China's thriving garment industry.

The next day I touch another side of China. Just an hour or so away by coach, Wuzhen is a recently opened cultural village. Here a group of us wander along flagstoned alleys, unable to resist peeking into living rooms just centimetres away. From some we hear the soft slap of mahjong tiles, from others the enticing smells of onion and things frying drift into the laneway. Some houses have converted their front windows into

筷子

impromptu shopfronts, offering passers-by bottles of water, handfuls of melon, hand-painted fans or dusty 'antiques'.

There's an unexpected Bed Museum which, in the snoozy post-lunch hour, seems highly attractive. Other places capitalise on tradition, demonstrating painting and the manufacture of calligraphy brushes, bamboo craft or printing and dyeing of cotton in the familiar indigo and white willow-pattern colours you can't help but associate with China. At one point we dodge streamer lengths of printed fabric hung out to dry from racks high in a courtyard.

As we climb the steeply arched bridges over meandering green canals and stroll along waterside lanes and corridors, it is obvious why Wuzhen is called the Venice of China, except that here the 'gondoliers' wear Chinese-style hats and do not sing as they pole their way up and down with their cargo of visitors.

Suddenly my guide's phone bursts into abrupt synthesised music. It's a few bars of Italian opera. Which one? I smile when I recognise it, incongruous, yet strangely appropriate in this country on the move. Ah, yes, of course! It's cranking out 'La Donna e Mobile'.

*Wuzhen: the Venice of China*

# 6. MY NIGHT IN A BROTHEL
## and other (sometimes sleepless) nights

*People have different dreams in the same bed.*
**Chinese saying**

'Did you Cherry Blossom your shoes today?' asks the voice on television behind me.

I am in Zhongdiang in south-west China, high on the Yunnan plateau and—although there's currently an ad break—Gordon is delighted he has been able to find cricket on the television here.

That is not the only entertainment. Music sifts in from outside and there is a group upstairs in a karaoke bar. We find these everywhere and hear rather than see them for ourselves. The noise—Chinese people in these sorts of venues are no better singers than Australians—as well as the smoke, keeps us away. Strangely, as at home, our hotel room always seems to be located directly over the disco or the bar, so we get to boom-boom-boom ourselves to sleep most nights ... if you know what I mean.

Many of the better Chinese hotels are government-run and cut from a template it seems. As poor Brian found, one lobby can look disconcertingly like another and the rooms and their ditto-ed amenities appear to be ticked off the same bureaucrat's master list. That said, I do like the luxury of the combs, razors, slippers and toothbrushes all laid out in duplicate so that when we arrive the washbasin area is already pretty well covered. I can't understand why in some countries I find one full-sized bath towel and two rather large tea towel-sized ones in a double room along with one shower cap and one face cloth.

Some places I have stayed in China leave a little to be desired. In one (nameless) city we stayed in a none-too-clean hotel. The carpet was soiled, the pillowcase looked as though it had been used and the bed was so lumpy and hard it was like sleeping on an uneven table. The peephole in the door was at giant's level, too high for me, so I pitied anyone younger or smaller. Regardless of these shortcomings, including a towel with a suspicious odour, it had more amenities than most five-star establishments, including the makings for a bubble bath. Unsurprisingly, the toilet didn't work when we arrived, but Gordon solved that, although others in our group maintained that nothing they did would fix theirs.

Gordon had discovered an old Elvis movie on a channel at the previous hotel, but here the television had about four stations—all Chinese—and there was the usual tuneless music blaring through the open window and mozzies somehow making it though the screens. While we have stayed in many worse places, the surprise was that externally it had appeared a much better bet.

In Deqen, on the border of Tibet and China—which is not a border if you subscribe to the belief that Tibet is now part of China, but I am not getting into politics here, just pinning the place to the story—we check into our simple hotel (think, rural accommodation in any country) to discover that we have been allocated a room on the fourth floor. Great! We really want to walk up a vast number of stairs, but at least we have no bags. They have been delayed somewhere else. At this higher altitude I find I can only do ten steps on the stairs then have to hang over the railing, gasping like a geriatric until my bloodstream fills with oxygen again.

On the first floor there is a sign, 'Welcome You'. We soon discover that the men's toilets are on floors two and four while the women's is on three. Helpful for Gordon, but not for me. They are very basic too. The loos are just slits in the tiled floor with a view over the town. Of course we must squat over them (more about toilets in another chapter), presumably providing a view for the town. There is a washroom next to them, but I plan to take a bird-bath and use the wash pan in the room. Luckily, there is a bucket and water, which is also meant for spitting and cigarettes, outside each room.

Our room at this hotel is clean with a sitting room/lounge, a television and a two-bed bedroom with quilt and blanket folded on the bed. Make it yourself seems to be the idea and here they don't give you a key to your room either. Girls on each floor will unlock it for us as needed.

As I look out our window over Deqen (pronounced Deshen and spelt differently in every book and map I see) it seems a real frontier town, a bit like the Wild West. So much so, I almost expect to see a shoot-out in the saloon or a gang fight in the main street.

Just as we are dropping off to sleep, there's a knock on the door and a call from the corridor. 'Come down and get your bags.'

Our luggage has arrived, so we hurry down to the foyer with its incongruous pictures of palms, sandy beaches and Niagara Falls. Then we huff, puff and—struggling for air yet again—hang over the railings up those four flights of stairs, poking our tongues out at 'Welcome You' as we pass.

Although we have slept in many places in China, one particular night I sadly forgot to blow up my self-inflating sleeping mat. I now finally realise what 'self-inflating' means: that I need to inflate it myself. At high altitude I don't have the lung-power available to donate any spare air to a mattress—that is if I wish to keep breathing independently as well—so I opt to lie there and think of anywhere warmer than Tibet.

This means I am in for a hard night, but I don't realise how hard. I am cold. Both my sleeping bag and mat seem to conduct the chill, rather than

筷子

insulate against the cold. I have cramps in weird places due to the acrobat-ics I did changing my clothes in our tiny tent. My neck aches, so does my shoulder, my hips and my back. I toss and turn.

One of the many possible side effects of being at high altitude is insom-nia, but I don't know if it is this or just a combination of the cold and my own discomfort. I have a deluded inspiration and get out of my sleeping bag to use it as a quilt for a while, but this is worse as now I have only the sleeping mat between me and terra frigidus (well, that's what I am calling it) and I begin to feel like I am trying to warm up Tibet with my body heat.

In Lhasa we stay in the aptly-named Yak Hotel. Here our room is deco-rated with amazing Tibetan art. The ceiling is covered with a rich tile-like design. There is a naive-style painting of a monastery on the wall and the frieze along the wall near the ceiling has curlicues and swirling creatures, flowers and branches and reminds me of patterns on old dinner plates when I was a child. The room even has lace curtains, topped by a pleated red, green and indigo ruffle.

Lace curtains! After our trek, they seem an almost decadent luxury.

Another time—still in the wilds of Tibet—our convoy turns in late at a long barracks-like building. We are at the door of our room when a man pushes in ahead of us and starts fiddling with the fuel stove. He doesn't speak, but then of course neither do we as neither of us has enough language to run a conversation, even an impromptu one that goes 'what on earth do you think you're up to?'

It turns out he's the official stoker for all the funny little peat-fuelled stoves in the place. They start these with fine strips of pine shavings, which we later discover come from the resident box-maker at the end of the row. He is so industrious that he keeps us awake until midnight with his sawing and hammering and planing.

This room, unlike some we have been in previously, has a hook that keeps our door closed, a light cord that actually pulls the switch situated at ceiling height without sparking and, while there are bare floorboards, there's even a jaunty scrap of curtain at the window and a bare globe overhead, so we feel quietly confident of both our comfort and security this night.

Which is better than poor Ian, also travelling in our group, felt a few nights before. Because of bad weather, we had been forced to stay in a place that was quite primitive, even by our adapted standards. Our guide cleaned the concrete toilet block some distance from our rooms before we were allowed to see them. Even so they would have been shut down anywhere else.

Like many, these loos were just concrete blocks over a pit and there is only one way you can use those for any sort of major loo-work. Ian told us the following morning that he'd had an irresistible need to use a toilet in the middle of the night. Not just for the standard, standing-guy sort of thing, for which he possibly wouldn't have needed to go as far as the toilet—it was that sort of place—but a serious undertaking.

The real disincentive was that the hotel compound was patrolled by several mean and mangy yellow dogs, that had howled their disapproval of us the moment we arrived. Ian thought long and hard before he finally gave in to this inconsiderate call of nature and made the trek across the court-yard. His description of his vivid fears while crouching there, his nether regions twitching at the thought of a possibly rabid canine attack, made us laugh till we cried. Strangely, Ian didn't seem to see it as quite so funny.

Now I'll tell you about the brothel. Of course, we did not know for sure it was and, I must say, no one ever admitted it either, but we believed it was and you can make up your own mind about it.

We had been travelling in convoy all day in our 4WDs, deep in Tibet en route for Lhasa. We were booked into what is called a hostel: simple rooms often used by pilgrims and very basic, as you would imagine. We had become used to these places, as we'd already stayed in several. Usually heated by a wood stove, the bedding was generally clean enough and the

筷子

thick, padded bedspreads meant we slept warmly. By now, I had found a way to sleep easier, without tossing and turning. Doubting the cleanliness of the pillows, I covered them with one of my T-shirts, turned inside out. That way, if the pillow was dirty, it affected only the outside of my T-shirt. Any face cream affected just the inside. I felt I had arrived at some sort of a win-win situation.

Here we are to share one room containing four single beds with another, older couple from our group, Wendy and Jack. As we are shown in, I notice a door at the rear with a bolt on it. I immediately slip it across just in case there is someone in the next room who might decide to take a walk into our room during the night and, who knows, steal some of our gear as they do.

In hotels I am always a bit suspicious of doors that open into other rooms from mine and can never resist giving the handle a jiggle to see if it's really locked properly.

Within seconds there is a terrible banging on the door from the other side and a torrent of yells. I take this as confirmation that the occupants of the next room are definitely not to be trusted and that I have cleverly stemmed a nocturnal attack by locking them off. The banging and yells continue, but no way will I open that door. I picture weapons and big people and call our tour leader for assistance or at least a translation.

She speaks through the keyhole, but there is no response nor does the pandemonium cease. Finally—and I think her very brave for this—she opens the door a crack. We see not burly bandits, but two wide-eyed young women, apparently deaf-mutes (which explains why they had not answered), their pretty faces painted and powdered. The sorry explanation is apparent to me. This is the poor girls' workplace. We have effectively been assigned to the brothel waiting room for the night.

I like to think I am fairly broad-minded, yet somehow I cannot face a night filled with a procession of clients tripping over our rucksacks—and perhaps rummaging in them too—as they wait for availability. Nor am I

筷子

up for the inevitable sounds that we might be privy to. Wendy and Jack would have been all right. They both depend on hearing aids and, once they remove them for the night, sleep soundly in blissful silence.

So I do the only thing I can. There is no other room for us to move to and, after checking that their small room, which has no other door, is equipped with all the creature comforts they need for the night, I mime the fact that I am going to lock them in again. They are to have a night off!

A little later there is a polite knock from their side. When we open the door one of the girls comes out glowering and marches through our room, apparently having decided to take her services elsewhere. A short time later however, she returns, happy this time it seems, to rejoin her friend in captivity.

Finally we make our way to bed, Wendy and Jack in the far corner because they won't hear any intruders, even if there are any, Gordon under the broken window next to the door, as he as the biggest and ... well, he's a guy. I take the remaining bed along the other wall and fall asleep.

At midnight there is an insistent knocking on the door. A male voice calls out waking me, but not Wendy and Jack, of course. Another male answers from our side: Gordon, gruffer than I've ever heard him.

'Get out of here!' to which there is no response, just a hasty scuffle outside as the man takes off, running by the sound of it.

Almost certainly, that needy gentleman did not speak English, but there must have been some subliminal male message there that sent him on his way in a hurry. Whatever it was, we had no more callers, all night.

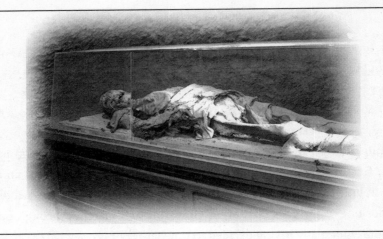

# 7. ANTIQUITIES

*Study the past if you would divine the future.*

**Confucius**

As we slowly negotiate the many steep stone stairs to the Yu Fong or Jade Peak Lama Monastery, our guide stops us.

'See there! This tree is 500 years old,' he tells us, 'It blooms twenty-one times every year, and bears more than 20 000 flowers in two colours. Every year.'

No wonder he is proud of it.

It's hard to imagine a camellia tree surviving for half a millennium, yet there it is. Its gnarled lichen-covered branches intertwine like a difficult puzzle. A Chinese puzzle, maybe, for here we are, near Lijiang, deep in the south-west of China, over 2000 kilometres from Beijing in Yunnan province, where not only the trees are old.

In fact, 500 years ago, during the reign of Emperor Chenghua of the Ming Dynasty, when this camellia first burst through the soil, Lijiang was already a bustling city, its government buildings in the eastern quarter 200 years old.

At the top of the monastery stairs, a dignified monk dressed in a crimson robe greets us, offering a platter of walnuts, apples and pine nuts, still in their brittle shells, accompanied by a saucer of fresh honey. His braid-trimmed cap is also red, pointed at the top like an elf's with triangular side flaps pinned up like impish ears. Silently and solemnly he presses his hands together and wishes us a gentle welcome. From his place on the porch the view across the gardens extends to a horizon of bare, folded hills, pale blue and green in the afternoon light.

The monastery is like so many we have seen already on this trip, dark and eerie when we step inside. Slowly, as our eyes adjust, the shadows resolve into prayer mats and brilliant silken patchwork wall hangings, long thin strips sewn together and pointed at the end, like so many neckties hanging in a cupboard. To one side the light of the yak-butter lamps flickering at the altar pick out the shapes of dusty scrolls and ancient holy books filed on high shelves.

Lijiang is home to the Naxi (pronounced 'nashi') people, originally nomadic herdsmen and one of the many minority groups in China. We're talking really ancient peoples here. Apparently the Naxi are descendents of the Kiang, who lived near the Huang-Ho River as far back as 2000 BC, although it's hard to imagine timeframes like this. Today the women wear broad-sleeved blue and white jackets with buttons and cords on the back, aprons and sheepskin shawls, for this area is high, around 2600 metres and the bitter winds whip their cheeks to a constant redness.

These people love to sing and dance. One night we attend a cultural show in the city and watch as a young man, dressed in a flowing goatskin vest and a woollen hat trimmed with hawk feathers, pipes music for the dancers. Nearby another plays an antique, single-string violin, its whining melody blending with the percussion and other string instruments.

A dance troupe of young women in long white trousers, topped by yellow-pleated aprons and red and white blouses, clap and sway. The

筷
子

braver tourists join in and try to copy the moves of the Alili, a famous Naxi dance. Most don't succeed.

Then a calligrapher comes on—the first time I have ever witnessed writing as a performance art—enthralling the crowd with deft pictograms from the Naxi's over-1000-year-old script. Only years later do I see something similar, in Kashgar, a man writing poetry on the street, using a sponge-tipped stick dipped in water. I don't know why, but I find it a most moving and beautiful thing.

Lijiang survived a crippling earthquake in February 1996. Our official guide, Mr Chi, giggles nervously and his wispy black beard flutters when we ask about the death toll. It was a big quake (seven on the Richter scale) and Mr Chi tells us that 300 people died in it. As an aside, he whispers that the figure was at least 1000. I later find somewhere else the toll reported as more like 2000, which still seems low given the town's current population of around 60 000.

About eighty per cent of Lijiang was flattened in the quake, a cultural tragedy, as this town has stood since Genghis Khan's son Kublai established it when he passed through in 1253 AD. Little wonder that UNESCO decided the year after the earthquake to preserve what was left and placed it on the World Heritage List.

Lijiang is officially known as Dayan Town meaning, literally, a 'great ink well', on account of the town's location on rich, river-fed flatland surrounded by green mountains. What remains of the old town is rich too, a mix of unusual, half-timbered or brick-and-tile houses with carved doors and painted windows, interlaced by an intricate web of canals and river tributaries, which in turn are crossed by innumerable timber bridges.

We stroll the cobbled streets, pausing to admire a brilliant skein of chillies drying in the sunshine outside a top floor window and say 'Hi' (well actually ni hao in Chinese) to an old man in a sheepskin hat, seated in a doorway smoking a slender pipe as long as his arm. Women rinse dishes in a canal as we pass and children peep out of shopfront doorways.

筷子

There is much to see around Lijiang too. It's October and the 'Grass Meadow' is carpeted with pink, blue, yellow and white wildflowers when we visit. At the bottom of a gorge, packhorses are saddled ready for trekkers, but our destination is the cable car, which rises abruptly about 300 metres so that, by the time we reach Snow Mountain Meadow at an elevation of 3100 metres, we are in cloud.

The official title is Jade Dragon Snow Mountain range. It's fifteen kilometres from Lijiang and, of course, looks like a gigantic snow-draped dragon, 5596 metres above sea level. Its thirteen peaks dominate the Lijiang basin and our guide tells us there are around 7000 kinds of plants to be found here as well as 400 types of trees in twenty primeval forest communities. It is a wildly beautiful place.

In spring, azaleas turn the mountainsides into an avalanche of brilliant colour. Wild ass, the Yunnan snub-nosed monkey, the lesser panda, a forest musk deer, clouded leopard, pheasant and a spotted, yellowish civet cat all call the Snow Mountain home.

Eight kilometres north of the city, in the ancient Baisha quarter, there are thirteenth-century religious buildings with remarkable murals that offer insights into Naxi culture. Mr Chi explains to us that the local people still have arranged marriages, but that often the young people run away or commit suicide, rather than marry someone they have not chosen.

Now here's a custom that could catch on. Women in this matriarchal society may choose seven or eight lovers and save their strength for more important things by calling in the 'uncles' to look after any resulting children who never know who their fathers are. Scientists are doing studies to see why there is no deformity or insanity from such possible inbreeding.

In this mountainous region, formerly home only to bears, deer and wolves, resort-style chalets and hotels are now opening up as skiing and tourism take over. At one stop someone passes around a card from a local hotel advising us that they have the added lure of 'heating beds'.

While I am grateful that the earth does not move for me while I am in Lijiang, I swear I feel a tremor. Things are on the move: new industries and opportunities, change, growth and stability, I hope. Yet, I know that some things will never change. That ancient camellia tree will stand, endlessly blooming and turning the ground beneath it pink with its petals. Foreve

Timelessness is something China seems to specialise in. Moveable type for printing was developed here hundreds of years before Gutenberg. Paper has been in use in China since around 100 BC, and where would old Guy Fawkes have been without the Chinese discovering the trick to making gunpowder (and ultimately fireworks) in the eighth century AD?

筷子

Then there is tea. The Chinese have used it in medicine for 4000 years, referring to it first in 350 AD, but it did not arrive in Japan until 850 AD and in Europe even later via the Dutch East India Co in 1609 AD. Of course, tea is credited to Emperor Shen Nung of China in 2737 BC. His accidental discovery resulted in tea becoming synonymous with China from then on. As recently as just over 100 years ago, tea-clippers raced from China to England with their precious cargoes and excited national interest. I guess they could have called it a nineteenth century World Cuppa!

As early as 3000 BC the Chinese cracked the code of silk making. It took the Romans, who loved the stuff and used it for everything from pennants to petticoats, almost another 4000 years to learn how. Originally they thought the raw silk grew on trees and ultimately they had to extract the secret from a hapless Chinese who they had captured. Even the navigational compass was developed by the Chinese and widely used on their ships by the eleventh century AD, well ahead of the early European explorers.

Also near Lijiang we saw a 500-year-old fir tree and another time some trees on the Ancient Silk Road with a sign affixed to them stating they were 1000 years old. I sometimes wonder how these living things are dated so accurately.

In fact, the Silk Road is rich with ancient discoveries. Every bulge in the earth just might signify the rooftop of an underground tomb. When walking in the mountains you might round a corner and find a twenty-metre tall Buddha carved into the cliffside or suddenly notice that a rock face is actually pockmarked with grottoes. On closer inspection you realise that the walls inside them are virtually wallpapered with frescoes of thousands of Buddhas.

At Urumchi, about as far north-west as you can go and still be on Chinese soil, our local guide appears a little nonplussed when he sees our itinerary. We are expected to spend the afternoon at the Museum of National Minorities and History.

筷子

'But it has burned down,' he blurts out.

Usually our guides are very adept at saving face and smoothly redirecting foreigners away from anything that might not be quite as positive as it should be, but clearly he has been caught off-guard. We learn that, about a year before, the museum had indeed been almost totally destroyed. Such a staggering loss for a city, yet no one has thought to mention it to our travel agent.

'But there is still something left,' he brightens, 'we will go there after lunch.'

So we find ourselves pushing open a gate that looks almost rusted closed and picking our way across the hot concrete driveway, webbed with cracks and tufted with dry weeds. Several of the buildings are permanently closed and I wonder when, or if, they will reopen. Even in China, it's hardly likely there is an endless and readily available horde of historical artefacts, numerous enough to restock a museum.

One block only, a low building, is open. A few staff are outside smoking, seated on plastic chairs, and they bound to their feet as we appear around the corner. The sign over the door reads in English 'Exhibition of Xinjiang's Relics, Treasures and Ancient Corpses'.

Corpses? Yes, that's what it says. Our guide has become more eager now, nodding and bowing.

'These are very important relics,' he tells us with pride.

As we enter the room, someone flicks on the lights. Throughout China we find this over and over—in shops and showrooms, museums and monasteries—electricity only used when needed, lights coming on just ahead of us and off again as soon as we pass, like a sort of illuminated Mexican Wave.

Not for the faint-hearted, this place, we realise as we step inside and see that the airtight glass display cases do indeed hold corpses that have been mummified by the hot desert sands of Chinese Turkestan around the towns of Cherchen and Loulan, where they had lain for several thousand years until their discovery just a few decades ago. It is believed the extremely cold, dry, salty surroundings simply dried them out, preserving them in near-perfect condition. Without exception the skin is parched dry and stretched taut across the bones, but many have still retained their hair and clothing. On closer inspection—once the inevitable initial shock of confrontation has passed—I begin to wonder if every last stitch of their ensembles has survived several millennia in the outdoors. Perhaps the museum's backstage personnel have entered into a little circumspect wardrobe consultancy.

The museum staffer who is following us like a shadow does not understand my supposition when I put it to her. She has other things on her mind anyway. Like making sure Gordon doesn't take any covert pictures of the corpses or knock into anything with the tripod he is carrying. He spends some time trying to convince her that, because he has the tripod and can use a slow speed for his pictures, there will be no damaging light from a flash, but the museum staff remain suspicious and adamantly refuse him permission. Maybe they want to sell postcards of their mummies. But why? No one else comes to this almost abandoned museum the entire time we are there.

However, these corpses are truly amazing. Here lies a male from Qiemo, 3000 years old, originally buried at Zhahongluk and discovered in 1985. His height is recorded as 165 centimetres and he has a round, bearded face, a high nose and wears a maroon robe, pair of very trendy purple and turquoise over-the-knee felt boots. Even now I can still see a sort of tattooing on his face. We are told he is of European origin, like several others here and all are believed to be part of early nomadic Celtic tribes.

Nearby lies a Qiemo woman, her fingernails still intact and dressed in a woollen gown. According to the plaque she is 160 centimetres tall and we are told she is of mixed race, Mongolian and European. She lies with her head slightly raised on a cushion and we can see her teeth through her grey, partly open lips.

筷子

A little baby who died between eight and twelve months of age, 3000 years ago, lies on its on back, its tiny eyes covered with two chips of blue stone. Beside it, touchingly, lies a milk-feeding vessel made by attaching a sheep's nipple to an ox horn.

In another part, there is a Hami ancient corpse, discovered in Wubao in 1978: a twenty-year-old European woman still curled up. Did she die in pain? Near a doorway lies a woman from Tiebanhe, called the Loulan beauty. She is not too lovely now, but 4000 years ago her deep-set eyes, high nose and chestnut hair must have drawn attention. She died at forty-five and we even learn her blood group was type O.

We spend some time 'meeting' these people, old and young, famous and unknown, all lying in state here. There is even a military general who died of TB and his wife, who outlived him by many years before she too succumbed to the same illness.

In fact there is a whole colony of these desiccated people here, gathered from many sandy graves and united in this place where, as luck would have it, they narrowly avoided being cremated as well.

筷
子

## 8. SKIP TO THE LOO

*If you bow at all, bow low.*
**Chinese Proverb**

It's the most popular dinner party topic when much-travelled people get together: 'You'd never believe the toilets in ...' and away the conversation goes. Squat holes, pits, the side of the road ... soon everyone has one better tale to tell.

Our Chinese guide, Tony, told us one of the best stories. A cultured Singaporean woman on one of his trips was like many people from that deodorised and sanitised island: ultra-fastidious. But of course the time came when she simply had to re-evaluate her ideals, lower her standards and use the side of the road for a pit-stop.

The possibility must have played on her mind. I indeed it became clear she had been thinking about it. To remain modest, she had equipped herself with a large sun umbrella and set it up cleverly to shield herself and conceal her activities, or so she thought.

What she didn't realise was that just below her, down the hill, was a primary school and the children, fascinated by such a bright umbrella in such an unusual location, trooped up to see what it was for. They stood around gaping at her as she squatted, one hand occupied in holding aloft what she had hoped would be her shelter and disguise. It acted instead much like the bright parasols used by tour guides to attract attention and marshal members of a group. You just have to hope she eventually recovered from the ordeal.

While recent trips to China, especially in the larger cities, have shown me that Western-style toilets are becoming more popular, in country areas I am often almost reduced to tears when entering a toilet block and seeing perfectly good—pristine, actually—white porcelain pedestal fittings with garden equipment piled all around them, a brick on the lid or the door locked closed and an official message—in Chinese, no doubt warning against its use—on the door.

Of course, while I may have serious doubts about the cleanliness of squat (and other) toilets, I believe many Chinese along with most Asians don't believe our toilets are all that hygienic either. I have stepped over drying corn to enter public toilets in southern China, averted my eyes from people happily squatting with the cubicle door wide open in others and, on the rare occasions I have found a proper sit-down loo, been amazed at the sneaker marks on the rim, because many Chinese still can't bring themselves to actually sit on the seat.

'How can you put your bott-um,' as one of our guides put it so candidly, 'where someone else's bott-um has just been?'

It's a fair argument, but I still have to come down in favour of the sort of loo I have always known. While I have never been one to leave my car in a disabled parking spot and despise those who do so without being eligible (I stop just short at crying out 'It's a miracle. You've been healed!' when I see them getting into their cars again as they leave), in countries like China, I am the first to charge into a toilet with that wonderful international blue and white wheelchair sign on the door. Why? Because I know that there will be a 'proper' toilet in there.

筷子

When you travel off the beaten track in China (which is almost anywhere outside five-star hotels) you can expect to use a toilet that is located at floor level. In many restaurants and other establishments that have had the money to install modern plumbing, this will be a ceramic plate with moulded places for your feet and, of course, the hole in the middle. Many have a hose and a bucket for washing away any mess and can be kept as sparkling clean as any Western toilet.

I have no idea of what the word is, but I love the Chinese symbol for 'Ladies,' which, out of necessity, I have memorised. It looks like two tightly crossed legs and is about as graphic a sign as I have seen anywhere. For ladies from a sheltered background (I speak personally here), perhaps the most confronting loos are the public toilets usually encountered in rural areas. The block may or may not have a door and, while the sexes are segregated, there are no cubicles, just a long trench with concrete on either side. If you are lucky there may be partitions, but generally not, so you all squat in a row and pretend it is all perfectly normal, which it is for about ninety-nine per cent of people using the conveniences there that day.

The Chinese seem to have a fetish about ceramic tiles too, so the entire walls may be covered in tiles, as well as the floors. In fact, in some parts of China, these oblong white tiles that we are more used to seeing in kitchens and bathrooms are used as a durable and attractive finish to the exterior of houses and shops.

Of course as you get further from habitation toilets can be much more rudimentary, ranging from behind a bush at the side of the road—or in open plains country behind nothing, although happily there is enough distance so that at least the short-sighted will not be able to see what you are doing—to a cornfield, as I was directed to use on a recent trip down the Silk Road.

I had been pleading for some time for a stop and our driver for some reason did not want to give in to my entreaties. No doubt he knew the status of the pit-stops and deemed them unworthy. I wasn't too impressed however about elbowing in amongst the dried-out cornstalks, many higher than my head, to a space that was out of view of the cars. It was quite clear too that I was not the first person to have needed to use this particular field.

'It's a good cornfield,' my driver laughed when I climbed back into the van.

Maybe.

Of course in more remote areas you can elect to walk on when your bus comes to a photo-stop and hope that the next curve in the road has enough shelter, but you have to be prepared to perform an impromptu pelvic floor exercise if something unexpectedly comes around the corner before you are through.

Most travellers, however, develop a philosophical attitude out of necessity. Do what has to be done, wherever and however you can and don't get too precious about it.

Me? My first Rule of the Road is: If you see a toilet, go to it. If you don't—as I have learned to my sorrow—you may experience many kilometres of teeth-grinding regret.

Despite this sound advice I missed one of the most scenic ones, mainly because of my gender. We were visiting the Potala Palace in Lhasa and Gordon needed to go. He was directed to toilets in a far corner of the

筷子

precincts. Anyone who has visited this imposing place will know that the palace is sited overlooking the city, so certainly it would have to have one of best loos with a view anywhere. What's more, he tells me, it was the longest, long-drop toilet he has ever seen. Maybe the Guinness Book of World Records should take a look too!

In his words: 'This is very much bloke talk, so ladies look the other way. My guesstimate is that there is a drop of some 120 metres from bottom to bottom. It is no place for the faint-hearted, prudes or those afflicted with epilepsy or vertigo. For a venue with such a low coefficient of friction, straddling this airy slot is a risky (or should that be risqué) business. It is the only legitimate toilet I am aware of where proceedings can be viewed from beginning to end in a single moment of time. One can be zipped up and far away by the time the last of your effort reaches ground. A unique experience, but make sure you drink copious amounts of fluid before visiting the palace and hang on till you get to the top floor or you will miss out on the fun. Okay ladies, you can come back in.'

# 9. DIGITAL CHOPSTICKS
## a word from Gordon Hammond

*When you drink the water, remember the spring.*

**Chinese Proverb**

I am standing with my trusty tripod in the onion market. It is not what you would describe as colourful, more a dusty green. The heavy odour of onion taints the air. I click off a few shots at random, peer into the review screen and wait. The smell of dust and onions seems heavier as the more curious close in. The surface of the screen is like a little mirror and I can see that behind me they have taken the bait.

Step 1. Stand back and let them see themselves for themselves. I can see Sally a few yards away employing the same strategy. With my team pressing close and watching my every move, I zoom in and take a selection of shots of the crowd around Sally. The sale of onions is experiencing a slump. Review time raises the interest to a new level of excitement as punters run back and forth from Sally's camera to mine.

Step 2. Using international body language laced with grunts, I ask permission to photograph the most striking subjects. Not a problem. I have earned the right to photograph my new best friends. These aren't mug shots. They're smug shots. I am stoked. I then realise that the feeling of elation is not so much that I have enhanced my collection of people shots, but that for a few moments our two very different worlds successfully merge with warmth, good will, fun and humour.

The rather irreverent and not particularly politically correct Monty Python song, 'I Like Chinese', had one thing right at the time when it was released: 'There's 900 million of them in the world today, You'd better learn to like them, that's what I say.'

There are a couple of simple ways of putting this to the test. One is to use a bush as the loo. Even the remotest 'relief squats' behind a bush in the wilderness of eastern Tibet aren't exempt from curious eyes.

The other way is to make a photographic tour of the country. There are Chinese everywhere. Millions of them and an amazing number love having their photographs taken. The rest have mastered the art of moving in front of the lens at the precise moment the shutter is released.

The more remote the area, the more fascinated the Chinese seem with the photographer, as he is with them. Whenever I clatter into view with my tripod and camera at the ready, along with various accessories stashed in my camera vest and bag, small crowds gather to make sense of this unusual looking foreigner. None of your discreet little miniature cameras, which characterise most tourists, when I hit the road. This specimen is different and worth stopping for.

If nothing else I bring a few minutes of light relief to the monotony of a hard day's work and they, of course, supply me with endless subject matter.

You wouldn't exactly call me tiny. I tend to tower over most of the locals who have not had the genetic and life-style advantages which have resulted in my added girth and height. I also become totally absorbed in my photography and am a disaster for anyone else who might want to take photos at the same time. I only have to look at Sally's pics to realise that the ubiquitous blot on the image is not dust on the lens, but her husband shaded under an Akubra hat, bent over his tripod, always on the hunt for that stunning shot.

Sally has a good photographer's eye, but she has a way to go in training me to stay out her line of fire. At least I can prove that I have actually visited these places, something that could never be established from the thousands of pics that I have taken. I may own a Japanese camera, but I don't use it as it was probably intended. On more than one occasion, I have stood in for the Great Wall, or a Giant Panda with people swapping places and cameras with each in order to have their photographs taken with this strange tourist in the background—me. That's how bad it gets.

However, I mustn't get sidetracked. Photographers are supposed to remain focused. Something happens in those absorbing moments whenever I have a camera in my hand: connection. I find Chinese people to be wonderfully warm and open. Maybe it is because I grew up in Asia and am very much at home there or perhaps it has to do with the simple, uncomplicated lives that many Chinese live. Either way, it is hard not to connect with them.

I am drawn to eyes and then faces and fascinated by candid portraits. (I can't help myself here, so let me give you a great photographic tip: whether people or animals, focus on the eyes and the rest of the image will look after itself.) Looking back through my hundreds of people shots of China one thing becomes patently obvious. The Chinese smile as quickly as you can blink. Not a contrived smile for the camera, which characterises so many Western facial shots, but a spontaneous lighting up of the face from the soul. Regardless of the hardship many experience in living in a tough country, there is a spirit of cheer and goodwill that characterises the nation. The comparison with India is very apparent. The desperate poverty and hopelessness, which is unescapable in India, gives little cause for joy. I have so many images of serious, sad Indian faces.

In China so much is happening with so many people in so many places. You know that while a picture is unfolding in front of you, another one is just around the corner. Sally, the true journalist, translates into words the sensory world of the living canvas around her. For me, time is of the essence. I move quickly and become totally engrossed in capturing a thousand moments, which can then be re-visited after the event on the computer screen. By and large the adage 'every picture tells a story' holds true. My life is so much richer for the thousands of stories that have been shared with me through the lens.

One day we are driving through a rural village on the road between Lan Zhou and Xiahe. For a few seconds we stop for the hay cart that has blocked the road. An elderly woman stands, warming herself in the morning sun. Great shot! The camera with my long lens is on stand-by. Wind the window down. Capture the moment. Move on.

Some of the gaps began to fill as the moment once again comes alive again on my computer monitor. She wasn't that old really, just lined and leathered from years of toil in sun, wind and cold. Her kindly face was framed in smile creases. Her hands were rough and fingernails dirty as she rubbed them together to beat the frosty cold of the mountain air. She stood in front of something she no doubt called 'home'.

Its walls were a combination of mud and straw with occasional panels of old bricks to give added strength. There was no door as such, just a featureless cotton sheet to keep the world and the weather on the outside. She wore a man's two-piece suit, drab, dark, colourless and dusty. The pinstriped coat was part of one suit and the baggy trousers borrowed from another. They didn't match and were no doubt salvaged from somewhere or other. Beneath her jacket was an under-sized, faded red cardigan. Its rough wool, large stitches and enormous buttons stretched vainly to cover the pink and white polo neck sweatshirt next to her body. The cuffs of her jacket and cardigan were neatly rolled to free her hands for labour. A pale blue Mao hat planted tightly on her head permitted only a few tufts of thin grey hair to escape its embrace. She may have stood in worn shoes on bare soil and been surrounded by wind-blown rubbish,

筷子

but she stood with dignity and self-esteem. Certainly no fashion statement, but this is one powerful image of a woman in possession of an inner strength and resilience.

Of course, not all of China is living on the edge of poverty. The country is on a roll and rapidly maturing economically and politically as it finds its way in a changing world. Cities, which appear as a dot on the map, are huge, crowded and polluted. They are full of contrasts and anomalies: rich and poor, ancient and modern, communism and capitalism, traditional and modern, religion and atheism. Contrast is one of the essential building blocks for the photographer and China abounds with it.

Probably no one group epitomises transition more than the young. The future of the country rests with this new generation who are the product of the controversial one-child policy. In spite of this draconian measure, there is an abundance of kids. That single child is the sunshine of the family. Indulged, pampered and protected as if the future of the human race depended on it. Of course, the parents are delighted whenever you photograph their little darlings.

Children are one of the most delightful subjects of candid photography and, as far as I am concerned, there is no better way to shoot them than when they are simply getting on with the task of being kids. Sadly, I have all but given up on photographing them in Australia. Pornography, paedophilia and photography are 'p' words that can too easily lead to another one: prosecution. I have a way of connecting with kids and have accumulated a wonderful collection of kid shots, but these days most seem to come from Third World countries. I am weary of looks from parents who regard me with suspicion.

Typical toddler. Tugging at her mother's arm and throwing a tantrum because she wants some brightly coloured whirligig, spinning, whistling thing being sold by an entrepreneurial hawker. No trip to the Forbidden City can be complete without one. A generation earlier the matter would have been settled with stern punishment, but this is a modern Beijing miss in her natty little black corduroy jacket, trimmed in post-box red with buttons to match, frilly white socks and shiny plastic shoes.

I can see that this apple of her mum's eye is already highly skilled at one-sided negotiation so I sit down at child level on the pavement, camera at the ready. There's got to be a picture somewhere here. Click! Awful face. Click! Still angry and awful. She looks up and sees this foreigner sitting on the ground photographing her outburst. It's funny, very funny. Click! The little digital screen assures me that I have the perfect photo of a China doll: a beautiful smile, head slightly cocked with two little pigtails on either side.

I beckon the two of them over and show them the image on the screen. Mum is tickled pink and obviously proud. The China doll giggles at being the centre of attention. We nod and smile for a few seconds and then it's all over. Everyone is happy. Mum is glad that the tantrum is over. The doll skips away having forgotten the thingamajig and I have a prize-winning photo.

I love the new technology of digital photography. For a photographer who specialises in people shots it is a brilliant invention. The little review screen is only 35mm wide but it is a remarkable people magnet.

筷
子

The strategy mentioned earlier seems to work anywhere and with just about anyone, especially monks. In both Tibet and the area known as 'Little Tibet' around the town of Xiahe there is no shortage of these austere, crimson-robed men and boys. Just as the average Irish Catholic family of a century ago consistently produced a priest or a nun to take their place in the hierarchy of the church, there is a certain status among Tibetans when their sons do a stint in a monastery. Before the days of Communism the country had a glut of monks, their excessive numbers creating unique social and political problems.

Even though the number of monasteries and monks has been drastically downsized, Tibetan Buddhism survives and continues to attract many devotees to the ranks of the monks. Many of these are mere children who enter the disciplined world of endless, droning prayers, dark temples filled with incense and candle smoke, hours of learning texts from sacred writings and a lifestyle which is far removed from the carefree days of my own childhood. I confess to being both intrigued and mystified.

Another component of a good photograph is show difference. We are curious about things that fall outside our day-to-day life and appreciate a different angle on a well-known subject. It is not every day that one has the chance to photograph Tibetan monks in their natural, striking habitat. Everything about them is very different. The buildings, fixtures, fittings and adornments rely on the use of strong, even gaudy, colours. These provide a wonderful background for the rich tones of the monks' robes.

This is the first real monastery we have encountered since crossing the border at Dequen. We are hundreds of kilometres from anywhere, having been on the road for days, seeing only the occasional nomad and not much more. We come around a bend and out of nowhere, there it stands before us. We stop in front of the white walls and wait. Within seconds there is stirring within; excited voices; running feet. The door opens as the monks hurry to investigate the visitors.

筷子

We have to keep reminding ourselves that we are the first Westerners to have travelled this particular road and that some of these people have probably never seen a white face before, let alone a camera and a video camera. The exposures come thick and fast, zooming in and out while the fascination is still young on their faces. I see the perfect shot. Step back a bit. Use this little path to get a low angle. Grab the long lens and zoom in. Faces with the monastery in the background. Pity no one told me that this was the local cess pit and I am standing ankle deep in unholy excrement. It is explains why they are all watching me so intently. My trusty tripod comes into its own as I gingerly extract myself from this slippery slope. Fabulous picture though.

These guys are so young. Just kids. Pimply-faced teenagers living in one of the remotest places on earth, far from the security and warmth of family and home. Clinging to each other for emotional support, the tall kid cannot let go of his mates. A large bunch of keys hangs from a rope around his waist. Why so many keys in a place which has few doors and no locks? I just cannot comprehend what their lives must be like.

Nevertheless we are alike in some ways. They love their sport, especially soccer. It's just a bit hard to tell whose side they are on as they all play in their robes. Their festivals and dances are fun times. I have a wonderful photo of monks watching clowns performing. Young and old, savouring the moment, wide grins lighting up their faces in obvious enjoyment.

As I said, the Chinese know how to smile. Sally captured a delightful moment with three monks leaning over my shoulder, vicariously taking photos with me then each peering into the review screen to give their approval of the finished product.

Even though I couldn't relate to their lifestyle, I had no problem relating to them, which just about sums up the thoughts of a photographer travelling through China. In order to create images which reveal the heart and soul of this wonderful country one must connect with its people and accept its paradoxes. This is a country that has been civilised

筷子

for millennia, yet still struggles to design a toilet. The people appear inscrutable, yet are delightfully transparent. The past and the present live side by side. You are very welcome, but never really belong ... unless you are Chinese.

'You'd better learn to like them,' goes the Python's song. Not a problem!

Footnote: The tripod, the traveller's companion has the following uses: a walking stick, cosh, something to lean on when listening to boring museum guides, essential weapon for beating off rabid dogs, a clothes line in hotels, a monopod, a salvage tool, balancing pole, something to hang a camera bag on, a sturdy support when using squat toilets and an invaluable accessory in producing consistently sharp pictures under all conditions.

筷子

PLEASE LUCK THE DOOR

## 10. EBGLISH NOT SPOKEN
### and other language difficulties

*Men's natures are alike. It's their habits that carry them far apart.*

**Confucius**

'Ebglish not spoken' reads the sign outside the mosque in distant Kashgar. It hardly seems necessary to try to say this. After all, here we were thousands of kilometres from Beijing, let alone any English-speaking country. Why should I expect my mother tongue to be in regular use?

Nevertheless all us smarty-pants English speakers come back with a list of the quaint and quirky phrases we see around the globe as people try to use our own so-difficult language. There's the sign in a park, in a city, in the middle of China where we found ourselves warned about **'No Spitting and No Rubbishing'**. Elsewhere we are instructed, in case we have the urge, **'Not To Write On The Trees'**. Luckily, we haven't (the urge) and we don't.

One of the best I've found is the framed sign on the wall over steps leading to a high temple at Tianshui, on the Silk Road. It gives a useful phone number, which I would include here if I didn't think people might make a nuisance of themselves using it. It simply says: **'Tourist Complaining Number'**.

筷子

This is almost as good as the one I covertly photograph at an airport, risking a swift visit to a distant room with a stern-faced official or worse. It points to a doorway and states: '**For Stuff Only.**'

At another airport, while waiting in line for immigration, I have time to read anything that's in English, which doesn't take long. Two signs, however, catch my interest and I copy them surreptitiously into my notebook...

> '**Enough inspection passageways shall be opened to ensure rapid clearance of passengers.**'

The second gives me even greater pause for thought:

> '**Frontier Inspection Standards**
> **The frontier station inspector shall enforce the law strictly and serve the passengers warmly during inspection.**'

In the city of Dali, the board outside our hotel says: '**Wellcame**' and advises us it has a '**carol okay hall**'. Yes, it takes us a moment too, to realise that's the place where people sing with a mike and backing tape.

'**Something Wrong, Ah... Painful? Come in Here please.**' Elsewhere, a massage and acupuncture clinic offers '**Hand Foot Paralysis**' massages and help with '**Constipation, Vomit, Tired**' and much more, including '**Camps, and Brokbone**', but optimistically promising '**Painful in, Happy out.**'

In the Golden Sun Hotel in Tianshui, I check the safety notice on the back of our bedroom door and find a:

'**Security Scattering Sketch Map**'.

**It reads: 'Declaration**

- **Please don't worry if a fire is occurring.**
- **We hotel have owned succor scattering facilities to sure you transmitted safely.**
- **Please follow the direction route to the information corridor and there safeguards will take you out to the security belts.**
- **Point profess your excellency seat.'**

(I think this last note refers to the 'you are here' dot on the diagram.)

Despite this, written English is perhaps the easier end of the language barrier. Speaking it must be so much more difficult as an exchange I had one evening in my four-star hotel made clear.

I wrote it down verbatim as it happened and headed it in my notebook 'High and (Almost) Dry in China'.

2pm: I pick up the service directory of my hotel and notice that hair dryers are available from the Service Centre. I am not surprised, I would have expected that. It is a top-class hotel, pompously named The Pearl and our twelfth-floor room supplies two toothbrushes, two razors, two combs and two pairs of slippers as complimentary amenities. Now this is more like it, I think. We have been trekking through wild areas where even a hot water tap would have appeared an unseemly luxury. Hey, let's face it, a toilet would have been excessive!

筷子

So here we are, finally returned unscathed to civilisation and the room has a door, with a lock. There is no brothel next door (that I know of, anyway) and the toilet has a seat and paper. Pure bliss! Surrounded by such civilised accoutrements I decide to wash my hair, of course.

5pm: I'll be ready in time for dinner, if I borrow that hair dryer.

5.15pm: I call the Service Centre. Extension 2002.

The conversation goes something like this:

Me: Hello, I would like to have a hair dryer, please.

Them: One of the several languages spoken in the region (I think).

Me: Do you speak English?

A muddle of sounds that could be 'Yes'. I hope.

Me: I need a hair dryer, please? Your directory says you have one to lend to guests.

Them: Can you spell it?

H-A-I-R D-R...

More incomprehensible words.

Me: Do you understand?

You want have dinner?

No...

Beep, beep... They have hung up. Great!

5.30pm: I make a second call, and find myself deja vu-ing instantly. I give my room number. I make my request, I spell hair dryer and I almost believe I have cracked the system, but suddenly I get suspicious. Is that a real person on the other end or a parrot? They are just repeating what I say. Ten-out-of-ten for mimicry. Zero for comprehension.

This time I hang up.

5.55pm: No hairdryer, so I decide to try another tack.

Ext 3002 Information.

Can it be there is only one staff person answering all those phones down there? I have an identical conversation. I plead, I spell, I offer my name and room number. I hyperventilate.

The voice, finally: You want wash clothes?

Me: No, my hair is wet. I want to dry it.

You like, you give clothes...

I don't want to give my clothes to anyone! Do you know what hair is? It is the stuff on your head. Mine is wet. I want to dry it.

Actually, my hair is nearly dry by now. I hardly need the thing anymore, but by now it has become an exercise in cracking the Sino-Anglo lingo barrier. I have been harbouring a suspicion that Chinese write English by merely transcribing foreign characters without any understanding of what they mean. Now I know they do. I couldn't help but wonder what other incomprehensible items they have in their service directories. Ones they pray no one will ever ask for.

5.56pm: How can you describe hair to a person over the phone? Short of running down to her desk and dripping onto the admissions register, I am darned if I know how to get my point across. I can't help it. I burst out laughing. Too bad if she thinks I am rude and calls down a pox on all my white relatives and compatriots. I'm out of control.

5.57pm: A nervous giggle at the other end. Obviously her fears about me are proving correct. I am a right nutto, after all. Then, suddenly—click. You can almost see comprehension kick in, light bulbs above the cartoon head—that sort of thing.

Ooooh! You want Hair Dryer! The last two words announced as if they had never come up before. What is your room number?

Me: (positively blubbering with relief) 1202.

6.10pm: A smiling boy appears at the door with a sparkling chrome 1970s-style dryer. Who knows, it's probably on its maiden appearance. I doubt if any other guests would have persisted this far.

There is one last hiccup. After discovering that the shaver outlet in the bathroom is defunct (no doubt sabotaged by the last person who failed to negotiate the loan of a shaver from the Service Centre) we compromise by not using the television while I dry my hair. It's okay so long as I

筷子

crouch under the table to use it. That way I can hold the plug in the power-point with one hand to keep it from falling out.

6.15pm: My hair is dry. Exhausted but triumphant I wind the cord around the handle of the dryer and leave it on the tabletop in plain view. I toy with the idea of calling the Service Desk to say I am finished with it.

I decide not to.

## 11. MADE IN CHINA

*The person who says it cannot be done should not interrupt the person doing it.*

**Chinese proverb**

'See there?' Jane, our Beijing guide is pointing out a tiny doll of a child, immaculate in her best lacy dress, a cap of ruler-straight black hair glossed over her round head. 'She is what we call a "little empress".'

The child stands regally on the steps of the Temple of Heaven, oblivious to her parents and grandparents fussing around her. We have heard about 'little emperors', the prestigious position that sons in China's one-child families enjoy, but this is the first time we have heard how girls are regarded.

Whatever your views on this radical step to limit China's population, the result is a generation of littlies who have grown up indulged and doted on. Each child has the full attention of at least two adults, but if the parents are also only children, then their respective parents will also be focused on this one small person. Six adults per child means plenty of presents ... and a lot of pressure to live up to their expectations.

Of course, many of the original 'one-child' generation are of an age to begin their own families. We are told that if two people who have each been the sole child of their parents marry, they may now have two children of their own. The pendulum swings.

Minority couples may only have one child unless they plan to move back to the country. In rural areas and among some minority groups this rule has not ever been as strictly enforced as in the cities, where a second child incurs a fine and no expenses paid for it or any further children. 'Some very rich people say "so what?" and pay it all without caring,' says Jane.

In rural Tibet there is always a scurry of dusty nomad children around us as we set up our tents. Even as we stop in some remote beauty spot to look back down over the endless hairpins we have just travelled, they soundlessly appear and surround us or pose artlessly, popping up in our viewfinders as we are about to click the shutter. Sometimes an older girl carries a baby in a blanket hung over her chest. On one occasion we see a lad of only about six carrying his hefty baby brother.

At one corner we come across a mother and son standing right on the edge of a glorious backdrop of snow-tipped mountains, looming over a turquoise river that crawls along the valley so far below. The little bloke is holding a turnip (I guess it's their dinner) so we take pictures of them and I give him a pair of gloves I have brought as gifts. I think they are cute, as they have little animals embroidered on the tips in bright colours, but like kids anywhere, he finds the attention is too much for him and starts bawling. Perhaps he thinks he might have to give me his turnip in exchange!

Strangely, throughout China, I have no feeling of claustrophobia, of being peopled out, as I have felt in India. In fact we are surprised at the lack of people much of the time, at the vast tracts of open land, forested areas, deserts and mountains. I had imagined it would be packed solid with people, standing room only, but China is so large that even though it has the world's largest population—1.3 billion as I write (but almost

筷
子

certainly more by the time you read this)—it ranks fifty-fourth in terms of world population density, with a modest 136 people per square kilometre.

Interestingly, Macau comes in tops with 17 600 per square kilometre because it covers such a small area. By comparison, despite what peak hour traffic might suggest, Australia is almost at the bottom of the list with just two Aussies to the same area.

In one small town in inland China, I am simply walking down an unpaved street, minding my own business—well, as much as any tourist does anywhere—when I feel a sharp 'ping' on the back of my legs. I swing around, but there are only a couple of children behind me, apparently playing harmlessly. I recognise them as the same little guys that Gordon had let look through his camera's viewfinder a few minutes before.

I continue walking, and there it is again, 'ping' on my shoulder blades. This time I am quick enough to catch them giggling as they stow their bright yellow plastic guns behind their backs. I sternly wag my finger at them and quicken my pace. I guess a broad Western back was just too much temptation.

筷子

It is not just the children who are intrigued by tourists. Again, we are well off the beaten track one day when we stop to watch some people working on the roadside, chiselling tombstones from marble. It seems hot, dusty, intricate work and they must have agreed, because they seem to welcome the chance to stop and inspect our busload of unusual visitors.

One lady is keen to meet me in particular and, more importantly, to feel for herself the flesh of my upper arms. She shyly approaches me, smiling and hesitant, then gently grabs my arm unable to believe, I suppose, that all of that could be real. I understand why when I see that her own arms under her light blouse are thin as rods and, I guess, just as strong. Satisfied with her investigation, she runs back to her family, giggling and saying something that it is probably better for me not to understand.

Once the stamp 'Made in China' was a signal that whatever the product, it would probably have been mass-produced and of inferior quality. Today, it more likely means that some enterprising clothing or souvenir company, located in another country, has realised that China has a massive and talented workforce which can satisfy orders swiftly and efficiently.

China, however, has been responsible for so much more. The sheer antiquity of the place is hard to comprehend. This is a country that introduced the world to gunpowder, silk, paper and so many other innovations.

Fireworks and gunpowder are of course two that most of us associate with China. Every Chinese restaurant opening features a noisy round of firecrackers to accompany the drums and dancing red and gold dragon. Did you know that gunpowder was originally intended to be the elixir of life? The T'ang dynasty's equivalent of scientists were aiming to create something that would make us (or rather the Emperors they were trying to impress) immortal, by scaring off evil spirits and devils.

Success would have established their survival too, but when you think about it, they created quite the opposite. While they were not entirely successful, they saved face by realising that this explosive substance, when packed into bamboo cases, went off with a satisfying bang, ideal for celebrations and ceremonies, many of which involved scaring off evil spirits and demons!

Of course this also meant they were in a good position, in the seventeenth century, to make the first bombs ever to be used in battle. For these too they used bamboo, only this time very wide pieces, which were packed with gunpowder and had a fuse inserted just as firework-makers had been doing for almost a thousand years with smaller rockets.

The magnetic compass was around a good 1400 years before it was perfected in the West, another major Chinese achievement and no doubt crucial to China's early maritime explorations. Originally intended for religious use, it was a little like the precursor of *feng shui*, developed so that builders could see if a house was aligned with nature, which in their minds meant correctly aligned with the true north, believed to be a propitious direction.

Currently there is a school of thought which believes that Chinese sailors in massive junks captained by eunuchs may have sailed halfway around the world, discovering America in 1421, some seventy-one years before Columbus made it. Thirty-one years, in fact, before Columbus was even born. This is possible, given the navigational head start they had. It seems they understood longitude some three centuries before eighteenth century English clock designer John Harrison did and had also perfected the rudder, all things that would have aided their journey.

Some believe that the Chinese also discovered Antarctica and beat Magellan by 100 years in circumnavigating the globe. Even Captain Cook may have to hand back some of his honour, as the Chinese quite possibly reached Australia 350 years before him.

These findings are only recently published, because the records have been lost for centuries, yet most of us have heard about some of the other major 'Made in China' discoveries and inventions.

筷
子

Originally something like a simple wooden disc with a magnetic spoon on top (the handle always pointing due south) the compass originated in the Qin dynasty between 221 and 206 BC. Fortune tellers had long used iron oxide stones or lodestones to set up their boards for foreseeing the future. Someone noticed that these stones always pointed in the same direction, and so these were crafted to become the spoon, and later a needle, on the compass. The first person to have used a compass for navigation was Zheng He, the man who led the expedition which is now thought to have discovered the New World.

The key to manufacturing silk was, of course, one of the finest Chinese discoveries and is credited to Lei Zu, wife of the Yellow Emperor of China, Huang Di who ruled in mythical times, around the twenty-third century BC. It is said she was idly seated under a mulberry tree (as you would if you were an emperor's wife) in the palace gardens and noticed silkworms spinning cocoons above her. With nothing much else to do, she started inspecting the fine, strong thread, winding some around her fingers and, delighted with its sheen and softness she wondered—to her servants and the court artisans, no doubt—if it could be woven into cloth.

For a thousand years after the Chinese began exporting silk to the courts of Europe the technique remained a mystery. Some Romans thought the raw material grew on trees and I guess they were half right. But none could ever guess that this gorgeous fabric—brilliant and shimmering enough to frighten enemies on the battlefield it was claimed, when the sun glanced off pennants made from it—came from a dull and pudgy grub.

So the Chinese, who had already been making silk for a couple of millennia and always the world's best entrepreneurs, transported this luxury across the often barren interior of their country and all of Central Asia where it sold for more than gold. The Silk Road grew up around it. Many other rare and exotic items piggybacked on its success too, as well as the interchange of culture and religion. When a sea-route to Europe

筷子

opened up silk went along for the ride.

Even today, Chinese herbal remedies are a revered and respectable part of alternative and mainstream medicine. The Chinese pioneered this too, using roots and herbs, tinctures and distillations to create a massive range, many of which are still in use, as well as a wine that acted like anaesthetic. Well, at least that's something still used today in the West!

Then of course, there's the gentle and apparently contradictory art of sticking needles into people so that they feel better. Acupuncture is believed to have been around for 4000–5000 years, maybe much longer. Some say 8000 years. In fact, the first book on it, *The Yellow Emperor's Classic of Internal Medicine*, was written about 400 BC. Acupuncturists originally employed stone needles, so we should be glad that we live in today's world where needles hardly thicker than a hair are used. In China, even today, operations may be carried out without anaesthesia, simply relying on acupuncture needles intercepting meridians to block pain.

While papyrus was used as long ago as 2600 BC in Egypt, the Chinese were the first—during the Han dynasty (206 BC–24 AD)—to make paper as we know it using silk rags, bamboo, cloth, hemp, mulberry bark, wood and plant fibres. The natural next step was to find the recipe for a durable ink then movable type for printing, which they did well ahead of Gutenberg. The Chinese printed the world's first book in 868 AD and by the end of the T'ang dynasty, 907 AD, there were bookshops in every city.

Once the papermaking process had been streamlined nothing could stop the resourceful Chinese. Despite its Japanese connection they claim to have invented origami around the second century AD, when wealthy people folded their letters into fancy shapes before sending them. Paper was also used for a number of other things: windows, children's toys, money, raincoats and umbrellas. There was even an industrial-strength paper used to make armour.

Clever tricks with paper still persist. On our last day in Beijing, Jane surprises us with a gift.

筷子

'Here,' she says shyly, 'I have this for you,' and hands us an envelope containing six tissue-thin, intricate silhouettes as fine as spider webs cut from coloured paper.

Industrially, China has always been way ahead too. The secret to casting iron was discovered around the sixth century and this paved the way for the first cannon to be built, which was then loaded with bamboo cases filled with gunpowder. Also devised was an iron basket, a sort of mini cannon that fired rocket-propelled arrows.

China's water-powered blast furnace was another key invention. They learned how to harness animals for use in agriculture and developed the simple yet superbly useful vehicle, the wheelbarrow around 2000 years ago, nicknaming it the 'wooden ox' because it carried more than a human could. More scientific was the invention of the clock, originally an astronomical device, with one version that has fortunately fallen from use. This was a giant water clock, designed to ring every fifteen minutes.

The Chinese are credited too—or rather an Emperor is, during the Yuan Dynasty (1271–1368)—with building the first planetarium. This was not a place from which to view the stars, but was enclosed. To view the map of stars on the ceiling, people sat in a chair hung from the inside of the dome.

Then there were the maths nerds who figured out the abacus. Visit almost any stall or small shop in China and sooner or later, if the calculations become difficult, the salesperson will whip out an abacus and click the rosary-like beads back and forth on the wires until they arrive at the result. To Westerners it makes no sense, but these simple mathi-magic helpers have been around since the second century BC and even today, if used by an expert, can prove quicker than using a calculator; andbatteries are not needed. In fact many believe that the Chinese also had a sort of decimal system in place 1000 years ago, developed to help people more easily remember the thousands of pictograms used in their language.

A Chinese child's toy—a spinning top that took off and flew for a distance—that originated in the fourth century AD was the inspiration for the twentieth century helicopter rotor blade.

Even more sophisticated was the earthquake predictor. Designed during the Han Dynasty, almost 600 years before the first Western sensor, the slightest tremor would set off a chain of events: a pendulum would dislodge a ball from the open mouth of one of eight bronze dragons positioned around a large pot and would tumble it into the open mouth of an ivory frog below. The device was designed so that people could easily see in which direction the earthquake was located by the position of the frog's back.

Unsurprisingly, bamboo featured in many early inventions. The Chinese figured out a way to process grain using bamboo machinery and also used it to make toys, baskets, paper, machines and even houses. The twin industries of silk making and the abundance of bamboo also aided the development of fans for women and soldiers, and kites for children.

In the home, noodles have been a staple part of the Chinese diet for centuries, although the jury is still out on whether indeed it was Marco Polo that brought their secret back to Italy, thereby planting the seed for the pasta industry. Regardless, the art of creating a skein of fine noodles by hand in just minutes, for me, has to rank as one of the most magical things that any chef can do.

Where would Chinese eating be at all without chopsticks? While today they are likely to be made from bamboo or plastic, over the 3000 years they have been in use they been made from bronze, lacquer, gold, silver or ivory, yet their plain-Jane name, Kuai Zi (Kuu-aye Tzu) translates simply as 'small piece picker-uppers'. While Westerners sometimes struggle with them, those who have used them all their lives can, without any trouble at all, pick up very small pieces—even a single grain of rice.

We will deal with tea in another chapter, but it would be wrong to leave the list of Chinese inventions without the most obvious one of all—

筷子

vital for serving tea, and every other meal: china. Bone china or porcelain is so closely connected to this amazing country that it even bears its name. Initially pots retained the white colour the clay assumed after firing, but around the thirteenth century potters began to paint their pots blue using the mineral cobalt. Even today, traditional Chinese china—think Willow Pattern—is often coloured blue and white.

Sometimes, when you look at China's contribution to the world and the number of amazing inventions the Chinese have contributed, it seems there was hardly anything left for the rest of the world to discover.

筷
子

# 12. TIME TRAVEL IN CHINA

*Be not afraid of growing slowly, be afraid only of standing still.*

**Chinese Proverb**

Several years ago, when I had the chance to visit Tibet, I quickly realised that I really should have done my homework. The problem was I hadn't spent much time doing any research about Tibet before we went. I thought I knew enough—that the country basically occupied a 4000-metre high plateau deep in the heart of Asia, and had been annexed some years back by China, an act which opened a Pandora's box of religious, political and human rights issues.

I did read up on altitude sickness (AS) however, and vowed to be super-careful as Tibet's major drawback is that the one sure-fire cure for AS—a swift descent to a lower altitude—can't be applied there.

I pictured meadows dotted with alpine flowers, wide plains stretching like the Nullabor on either side. I saw myself sipping yak butter tea and snacking on barley meal tsampa while chatting amicably (via sign language of course, I wasn't that naive) with husky nomads while seated in their smoky black tents. I had never met a yak.

The reality gobsmacks me. For starters you don't just arrive in Tibet. However you approach it, you come at it slowly. From the south via Kathmandu in Nepal or our way, from the east via China. Even though we fly as far as K'unming there are still many days of bus travel through 1000 kilometres of western China before we reach the border.

At Dali, 400 kilometres beyond K'unming, we see sunflowers: giant ones with centres as big as bread and butter plates, packed with seeds like matches in a matchbox. We watch people harvesting rice too, shaking the heads first then stacking the remainder into pagoda-shaped haystacks.

The process seems to be that the women plant the seed then cut the rice when it is ready. The men feed it into a thresher—some pedal-driven and others with a motor—right in the field. The women take the threshed stalks, tie them, put them into stooks and finally haystacks. Ultimately this hay is burned and the ash used as a fertiliser, as the binder in adobe bricks or as stock feed.

After the grain is threshed the whole lot is put into bags (by women of course), carted off to be winnowed and ultimately spread out to dry on concrete slabs. Chillies and corn are dried that way too, although the tobacco we see is mainly hung over poles. It is said the people from the mountain areas smoke heavily because the odour goes through their skin and scares away the snakes. Later we see buckwheat growing too, its dainty white flowers icing the hillsides.

Under some Government initiative, our guide tells us, each Chinese citizen is meant to plant two or three trees every year (if they do it at three billion or so trees a year, China will soon be one immense forest). To us it seems most of them are gum trees. We pass them growing all along the roadside making a nuisance of themselves, especially when we want to photograph scenes as the bus goes along. Tony cannot pronounce eucalyptus, but we persevere, making him learn to say it and without once telling him that he can just as easily call them gum trees.

We pass women working on some new stretches of the road, cracking stones.

'Before women's liberation, women have no name,' says Tony. 'They use their husband's name when they are married and when they are widowed they become so-and-so's mother only. But now, the guys are hen-pecked.'

As we head west the ripe rice is golden against the green of the stalks and the blue sky and misty air blend into infinity. Later fir trees and rhododendrons and, finally, a magnificent plain on the eastern side of the pass. It reminds me of the open central area of France, the Auvergne, only there are rice paddies here with scalloped terraces, like receding wave patterns on the seashore.

We spend days among the mountains. At one point, as we look down, we can see pockmarked meadows where presumably nomads have camped. Later we see burned out camps with only the stone walls left standing and a sort of turf growing around them. Little puffy clouds soften the snowy horizon and there is snow much closer, on the fir branches at the roadside.

'There is Mei Ling Snow Mountain,' says Tony, pointing out this virgin (unclimbed) mountain. 'It is a holy mountain and over 6774 metres. The highest mountain in Yunnan.'

筷子

The Tibetans walk around it and believe they will be blessed, he tells us. Apparently some Japanese tried to climb it once and nearly reached the summit, but received an incorrect report that there was a storm coming. They went down to find that the information was wrong and the weather was still clear.

We switchback around mountains that appear again in the valleys, like interlocked fingers with a cuff of white at the end. Finally it seems that Tibet can not wait any longer and simply came to meet us. We rumble up one side of a mountain—flanked by typically tiled and painted Chinese homes—to emerge at the top in a foreign land. Hay is slung out to dry on huge ladder-like racks that punctuate the plain like giants' easels outside each village.

We stop once to collect wildflowers—wild anemones, daisies and other little things—and, finally, we are beyond all the slit-like gorges and over the top. Instantly the terrain changes: red and gold-leaved tiny shrubs dot the flat grassland. Purple flowers provide a colourful backdrop for the yaks: huge moth-eaten looking black beasts with cruelly sharp horns pointing upwards. I will do everything in my power, I decide, to avoid being the object of a yak attack. As if on cue two small boys controlling these massive animals with feeble flexible poles, shyly come up to me and say *Tashi delek* (Hello).

There are women too, red scarves wrapped around their heads and over their mouths, peeping from their whitewashed houses made from a sort of adobe plugged between uprights, but with the walls leaning inwards at the top—presumably for greater strength. The gabled roofs— each sporting a forked branch of twigs and a ragged fluttering blue and white flag scrap—lack the curved point on the ends that we have become used to with Chinese houses. Wooden shingles are tied on here instead and simply weighted down with stones.

These Tibetan faces though are the real key to the transition: almond eyes, cheeks scrubbed raw by the brutal climate, long lustrous hair and brightly woven cloaks and aprons with patterns echoing the decorative bands painted at the rooftops of many houses. These are not Chinese faces. If anything they and the architecture hint at some mystery migration from South America, who knows how long ago.

A good day's travel beyond the place where we first sensed the beginning of Tibet, we reach the official prayer-flagged border-pass cloaked in smoke from a mess of shrines. Despite its significance there are no border formalities. We simply move our belongings from the Chinese bus that has brought us thus far, meet our new drivers and guides and swap into battered 4WDs for the rest of the journey to Lhasa.

If the Tibetan people jolt my preconceptions, the countryside sends my notions sprawling. Rushing mountain streams, strewn with boulders the size of railway carriages, lazy turquoise rivers and massive chunks of turquoise—the real stuff—braided into the women's long dark hair and sewn onto their clothing. I certainly didn't expect to feel like I was part of a postcard, day-after-day, either. Yet, as we bump along in our 4WDs, sometimes hundreds of feet above almost sheer drops, we gasp, not only at the inevitable consequences if the driver misjudges a bend, but at yet another jaw-dropping panorama.

Not that it all is dead easy. First there are the toilets—or lack of them. Towns at least have squat toilets or maybe a trench with the expectation your feet will span the chasm. On the road you hope for, but don't expect, a bush or a rock or a even a simple curve in the road.

Then there is the above-mentioned altitude sickness, not to be trifled with. It could take days to judder across the plateau and down again. The only treatment is prevention—lots of water, slowly, slowly as you go—which isn't as hard as it sounds. We find ourselves moving like invalids as we puff up the inevitable flights of stairs at our hotels, gasping for air.

Yet, these are minute inconveniences as we travel through a country awash with superlatives. Snowy passes underlined by fluttering red, green, yellow and blue prayer flags are cause for our Tibetan driver to whoop in thanks as we finally, safely, attain each summit.

筷子

Keyhole glimpses, through fir forests, of sometimes still unconquered mountain peaks which chomp jagged pieces out of a sky too blue to believe, huddles of nomad tents in deep valleys or open-sided buses crammed with cheering school children become commonplace. So do multi-storey monasteries glowing serenely on the hillsides in the morning sun, yellow and maroon-robed monks silently going about their tasks in the courtyards. Elsewhere we see yaks hauling a crude wooden plough and the simple, timeless act of a man lowering his yak skin coracle into a river.

Our Tibetan driver knows just one word of English: 'Stop!' and he reacts immediately, uncomplainingly skidding to a halt each time so we can take yet another picture. Unperturbed, he simply squats on the stony roadside, lights up a cigarette and waits for us ... and for a nomad visitor. It seems we can stop anywhere—even the day we travel through a snow-storm—and within moments a nomad will appear from his just 'off-camera' tent. Patiently they pose for us, smiling: always smiling, always helpful and just as curious about us as we are about them.

Tibet retains, often against all odds, its Buddhist religion and we sweat up hundreds of stairs in monasteries, amazed at the monks' piety and their simple life. How they can sit, chant and pray for endless hours, and still smile benignly I will never know. We carry torches as the glow of yak-butter lamps scarcely illuminates the gloomy interiors, glancing hesitantly off the ornate gold embroidered hangings, shelves of dusty scriptures and maroon and gold cushions and mats, as if unwilling to disturb the meditative mood.

The pivotal point of our trip is of course Lhasa, Tibet's capital, which—at an elevation of 3700 metres—is one of the world's highest cities. Interestingly its annual average hours of sunshine (3600) almost matches its altitude. Here there are even more monasteries and prostrating pilgrims. Some have inch-wormed their way to this city for hundreds of painful, stony kilometres. It's an incomprehensible web of dusty market streets with more people than we have seen since the border ...

in total. Here the thirteen-storey, maroon and white Potala Palace with its 1000 rooms, rises supreme above the city, dominating and defining it as if its imposing bulk is also a fortress against the erosion of other ways, other practices.

Westwards the country becomes increasingly barren and bleak with the beauty more commonly pictured by most people when they think of Tibet. These are the snapshot scenes of brochures, especially those outlining trips from the other direction, through Kathmandu. Few travellers are lucky enough, as we are, to see Tibet's eastern side, its forested grandeur. I feel both amazed and ashamed at my previous, king-sized ignorance of this region.

They say that when you return from high altitude you feel wonderful because of the effect the rarefied atmosphere has had on your body. And yes, I did feel great. So I should have, for I had been privileged to be—literally—on top of the world.

All my life I have dreamed of travelling the Silk Road. The name has enormous mystique, and I longed to go and see it for myself. When we learn that Gordon has won a photographic contest and the generous prize is a trip for two, including fares and all expenses, suddenly it is possible. After I finish congratulating him, I enjoy my own moment of celebration.

Once upon a time, long, long ago, when silk was used for pennants instead of petticoats, the Silk Road was a dirty and dangerous place. As I begin to learn about the route I have to realise that this is not—and never was—just one road. Rather, it always branched: north, south and central, seeking mountain passes and safe passage, skirting the worst of the deserts before striking out over central Asia and branching again, north and south.

Nor was silk, first produced in China in 3000 BC, the only merchandise carried at great risk and cost along those 7000 kilometres. Paper, furs, jade, ceramics and gunpowder also made the journey westwards.

筷子

In today's markets, in cities along the route, rolls of silk are almost lost among towers of embroidered hats, cartloads of watermelons, shoes, fans, handbags, paintings and spices ... and tragically, fox and cat skins and pelt after pelt from dozens of endangered species, but more of this elsewhere.

Maybe it was always this way, the silk jealously guarded until it reached the courts of Europe. So enamoured were the Romans by this lustrous fabric that they paid its weight in gold. The ladies of the court loved the sensuous, slippery feel of their new garments. It was centuries before any other culture cracked the seemingly ludicrous secret of spinning its thread. As long as China held the patent, the rest of the world was its willing customer.

We travel the Silk Road the easy way—in 4WDs, trains and cars—but even so the route is tedious. Leaving the Turpan to Dunhuang train we learn that we have crossed the Gobi Desert in our sleep (at least a far-flung corner of it), but we spend many other hours driving over treeless, featureless plains, through 'black mountains', which resemble giant slag heaps of cinder-coloured rocks. Others are bare and as bright as fire.

Around the Turpan basin—the world's second lowest place at 155 metres below sea-level—the average summer temperature is 47°C and the annual rainfall 200mm. Those first travellers must have almost given up at the enormity of the trek—several thousand kilometres gone, several thousand to go—slogging through these wastelands. Turpan has been called 'the lowest, hottest, driest, sweetest place on earth'. The first three are easy to understand and the sweetness is due to the grapes that are grown and dried here.

The early merchants stocked their caravans of camels, horses and mules with enough to sell and barter along the way to finance the journey, mindful of bandits who might so easily cream off their hard-won profits. Today's Silk Road is crammed with new age camels—lumbering semis and faded blue Dong Feng trucks, laden to the limit.

Perhaps the prize for the Silk Road's slowest trip must go to the trail-blazer, Zhang Qian, who, in the second century BC, was dispatched from X'ian by Emperor Wu-Ti. His brief was simple: see what lies to the west, decide if it is of use to us and bring back your report.

He was soon ambushed and jailed for ten years before escaping and resuming his mission to discover amazing things: 'horses as swift as light' he said, 'and strange peoples'. The hapless scout turned for home, but as luck would have it, was again captured and imprisoned. Many years after leaving the king's court he finally returned with his tales. The emperor was impressed. The Silk Road would begin.

X'ian—its name meaning 'western peace', 1165 kilometres south-west of Beijing—is commonly seen as the commencement of the Silk Road. It was the ancient capital of China until the end of the Tang dynasty and once vied with Rome and Constantinople for title of the world's greatest city. Its fourteen kilometres of walls are so broad at the top—fourteen to fifteen metres—that people hire bikes and cycle right around.

'There was a vote in 1949 to see which should be China's modern capital,' Shelli, our local guide tells us, 'X'ian came in just two votes behind Beijing.'

The 6000-kilometre Great Wall, stretching to the coast east of Beijing, was originally built to prevent marauding northerners from knocking off the goodies that had been exchanged for silk. The return journey was possibly even more perilous, for now the baggage held spices, glass, gold and ivory. Knowledge of Buddhism and other cultural trends also hitched a ride with returning travellers.

In Kashgar, on the far western border, one dusty morning at the local livestock market, with nary a Western tourist in sight, we are surrounded by the local Uygur people. Their heritage is from Central Asia, due most likely to those ancient traders and showing in their features. Some even have the blond hair and blue eyes of parts of Eastern Europe.

As we mingle with the modern-day traders a cart, drawn by a newly

筷
子

purchased horse and carrying a brightly dressed family, races past. Elsewhere camels snort and fidget on their ropes, as they would have done here 2000 years ago.

An hour's flight north of Kashgar, Urumchi is another key city on the silk route. Today it is the most inland city in China, some 3270 kilometres from Beijing. It would be three hours behind in time, except all China uses Beijing time, so dawn is very late here. By contrast, Kashgar, even further west, sensibly does its own thing and sets its time two hours behind Beijing, which makes sense as in reality it is nearer to Moscow than China's capital.

East of Urumchi we visit the aptly named Heavenly Lake, halfway up a mountain, shimmering in the morning sunshine and watch as tourists pack onto ferries for a lake tour or dress up in the bright, flowing costume of the local Kazak people to be photographed against a backdrop of the lake.

That is another of China's Silk Road surprises. Minority groups merge and mingle as we traverse the country: Kazaks, Uiygurs, Tibetans, Han Chinese, each with their own intricate history, language, religion, clothing and food.

Ah yes, the food. Our tour allows us to slowly work our way back from Urumchi to X'ian, as did those original traders for 1500 years until the land route gave way to a sea passage in the fifteenth century.

In Urumchi and Kashgar our meals are mutton based, Muslim and delicious. Further east, in Ganzhou, they become spicier and in a Tibetan restaurant in Lan Zhou we marvel at an amazing twist on simple fried potatoes. In Tianshui we find a dish that we declare to be one of the most wonderful things we have ever eaten, but more of that in another chapter.

Religious places of worship along the Silk Road morph from the amazing mudbrick Sugong Minaret near Turpan—which stands like an extravagant sand castle dominating the bare land—to a brilliantly enamel-tiled mosque at Kashgar. Buddhas are carved into the rock face many metres

筷子

high at the Thousand Buddha caves at Binglingsi, near Lan Zhou. So many places, so many Buddhas: painted on walls, carved and hidden in grottoes and caves, ranging from plain clay and doll-sized to massive and gilded.

Each day holds a dozen surprises. In a museum in Urumchi we gaze at the 3000-year-old human bodies perfectly embalmed by scorching desert sands. At Crescent Moon Lake near Dunhuang, we discover an unexpected oasis amongst towering Sahara-like dunes. We visit the crumbling remains of the 2000-year-old cities of Jiahoe and Gaochang, now abandoned to the desert winds, and days later the intact fortifications of Jiayuguang Pass at the western end of the Great Wall.

The terracotta armies in the walled city of X'ian awe us, of course, but so does a lesser known display of Lilliputian figures from recent excavations at nearby Hanyangling, discovered when the airport freeway was being constructed in 1991. The museum was only opened in early 2004, but the estimated 30 000 half-sized figures are every bit as fascinating as the warriors. They are naked now. The silk clothing and armour originally made for them, as well as their wooden arms, have disappeared, but they are anatomically correct. Even their pigs, sheep, cows and chickens accompanied them here, as well as daily necessities such as coins and weights.

In just over three weeks we have only scratched the surface of this amazing route that has always done the impossible: allowed travellers to move through time as well as distance. Maybe, after all, that is one of the Silk Road's greatest surprises.

# 13. CHINESE TAKEAWAYS

*If you are in a hurry you will never get there.*

**Chinese saying**

'Oh Jimmy!'

It is an involuntary exclamation as our 4WD bounces, jolts and shudders on the endless corrugations, almost shaking my teeth loose. Then it hits a really big one. We're wedged tightly in the back seat. My hipbone has created a permanent dent, I reckon, in the door panel, but this latest sudden bucketing rips a protest from me.

It is not the fault of our driver, Jimmy, of course. His driving is actually excellent and he controls the vehicle with great skill, born of years of practice, as it skitters like a wilful mare on this loose gravel. Already on our trip into Tibet he's negotiated landslides where I was sure the stone falls would stop us, but he somehow edged around them and kept going. He has forded streams of icy grey water rushing over green stones, squeezed past a broken down vehicle that almost filled the track and dug us out of a sticky black bog shortly afterwards. Somehow too, for hours he found his way across a glary, snowy wasteland with no signposts.

This is all part of the routine twelve to fourteen hour day of driving on our trek. He and his co-drivers also help put the food out at lunchtime, if we are picnicking, then cook dinner for us at night when we camp. They pitch tents, dig toilet holes and are up first thing to bring us a basin of water for our early morning toilettes, before they prepare our breakfast.

So ... in my eyes he is not only a good driver, but some sort of super-human, especially when I consider that he and his colleagues made this trip from Lhasa just the week before in order to meet us at the Tibetan border, where we left our Chinese bus.

Jimmy does not speak English, so he leaves us in the back seat and Dorothy in the front to amuse ourselves. When he hears his name this time he swings around, alarmingly and looks me straight in the eye. I cannot tell if he is surprised, angry, anxious or simply wondering if we need him to stop. Does he think I doubt his driving skills? Is he fed up with me for my apparent fear? The moment goes on and on, it seems. All the while, of course, he is still driving, still skipping across those unreli-able stones, still mere centimetres from the edge.

Many people feel that a trip to Tibet is an intensely spiritual experi-ence. They mean, of course, the visits to monasteries, their ageless build-ings wrapped in an almost palpable faith and the example of the monks and novices devoting their lives to religion. While agreeing with their sentiments, my response is even more basic. After travelling for days on roads where every hairpin turn reveals an even higher view of a valley hundreds of metres below and the mouth-drying experience of looking down and realising that the distant vein of turquoise is indeed the bustling river you crossed just an hour before and that the slightest misjudgement by your driver will have you plummeting back down there ... then you pray. I have never prayed as much as I did in Tibet.

The drive today has involved a road hanging almost exclusively off the side of a mountain and which, when seen from a distance, is a tiny zigzag

筷
子

scribble. When we see it rising forever to a snowy horizon, we say 'no way!'. After far too long with our eyes locked, Jimmy turns back to the wheel and my heart resumes beating with a mighty thump. I don't make a sound for at least an hour and never, ever call his name again.

Days later we see vultures, rising, dripping from another river, this time much closer. It is a steep fifty metres or so below us and these birds have been diving there in the frothing emerald torrent littered with rocks. Their massive black bodies gleam in the sunlight as they heave themselves away and upwards then flap down to rest in a field beside us. The drivers are excited and jabber to each other. 'What is it?' we ask. 'What does it mean?'

'A bus went over there two weeks ago,' they tell us finally. 'Twenty-eight people were on it. They are still in there.'

While driving in these remote parts may seem scary, the cities add another perspective to getting around in China. The sheer number of vehicles causes us to panic.

'Do you drive here?' we ask our guide in Shanghai and he answers almost before we finish our question.

'No, never. I always take a taxi.'

While the larger commercial cities, such as Beijing and Shanghai, are thick with taxis, the adult population in other centres is still doing the inevitable bicycle to motor-scooter to car progression evident in many Asian countries. In Chengdu our hotel window overlooks a fragment of open space below, packed solid with parked bicycles. At the traffic lights hundreds more jam the front position, wheeling swiftly away and weaving between the equally dense swarm of pedestrians as soon as the lights turn green.

We make the mistake, just once, of sitting in the front of the hotel transfer vehicle sent to pick up our group from the airport. It is great position from which to turn and snap a picture of our group, waving heartily, but if I were to swing the camera around, I would capture a much more startling one.

We have driven, in country places in Australia, through swarms of locusts or grasshoppers that beat head-on into the front of the car and the windscreen. This traffic is like that. While, of course, none of the oncoming vehicles actually make contact with ours, the visual effect is the same. Trucks, buses, bicycles, cars, big and small seem magnetically attracted to us, leaning away a millimetre at the final moment, before they would certainly hit us, then closing again like a tide behind us and whatever else is going our way.

That there is no confusion is equally amazing. This is simply a normal day's driving: a slow yet potentially deadly dance that relies on goodwill and steady reflexes. Hardly a horn toots and no one (except me and, for the first time, I see Gordon flinching too) seems at all perturbed. Maybe it is all those years of early bike riding.

For a country so concerned with longevity—eat your cabbage, wear jade, avoid sleeping with your feet towards the door—the attitude to driving here is a real Chinese puzzle. Consider this. You are bumping down a rural road headed straight for one of this country's ubiquitous blue Dong Feng trucks. It's loaded with rocks. You are bouncing around in the back seat of your guide's 4WD. There is a seatbelt of course, but like almost every other vehicle you've travelled in, there is no buckle end. It has long ago burrowed deep into the upholstery.

'We don't need,' your guide has told you. He is entitled to say that because he is in the front seat and has to wear the seatbelt.

The truck is hurtling towards you. Metres from impact a flick of someone's little finger lightly guides the wheel and you breathe again. Just one episode like this in Australia would have you ringing friends that night, saying, 'I had the closest call today. This idiot...'

In China, you can expect a dozen near-death experiences in five minutes and that's just when you're on four wheels. Pedestrians face even more enormous risks. When I have to assume that role and need to navigate some choked intersection I attach myself, child-like, to a local adult and match

筷子

them step for step as they cross. If there is no adult I'll go with a youngster, anyone, as long as I can trust them to get me to the other side in one piece.

Gordon has other advice: 'Just get their eye,' he says, meaning the drivers or cyclists. 'Move slowly. Don't run. Keep a steady pace.'

In Beijing we watch as mothers transport their children to school on bikes, the girls like little dolls, beautifully dressed with hair immaculately clipped by plastic hair slides or tied with ribbon, the boys sturdy and confident. Someone points out a 'pregnancy bicycle'. It has three wheels and a little seat on the back. I see the result of one of those pregnancies, strapped on the seat of another one.

Elsewhere the motorised vehicle drivers are crazy, just like in Sabah and Sri Lanka, I feel. They do amazing things, such as overtaking between two passing trucks and it is surprising there are not more accidents. We see one though, involving one of those strange, double-decker sleeper buses and there are many close calls.

At times when we are in slower vehicles on the open road the trucks rumble past blasting their horns all the time, whether they need to or not. Apparently, the law is that you must sound your horn if it is likely you could hit someone, otherwise you can be charged for negligence. If you've been killed, however, how do you prove whether a horn was sounded or not?

On one trip we see a portion of the Burma Road that is being turned into a toll road. It is an amazing feat of engineering and we stop for a while to watch, amazed that so much of it seems to be done by hand. We see men scrambling up the sheer sides of the embankments, most of which are shored up with breezeblocks and between which they are planting grass to further stabilise the ground. Elsewhere women labour, cracking stones into shape to form the sides of these massive walls. China is on the move and every newspaper trumpets the construction of a new superhighway from one major city to another, but few consider the human industry behind it.

The vehicles we see as we travel through much of rural China are fairly much the same: blue trucks with dirty canvas covers, jeeps, sleeper buses, people-movers like ours and only a few cars. Many locals use funny little plough-trucks that double as buses carrying up to twenty people at once. There are also bikes, motorbikes and horse-drawn carts. Somewhere we see one poor horse pulling a cart of logs while its driver whacks it continuously. Elsewhere we sight apparently self-propelled haystacks, which turn out on closer inspection to be mounted on bicycles or motorised carts. How the drivers manage to see through their blurry load is a mystery.

Animals are valuable for transport in China too, as the distances stretch out. We saw plenty of buffaloes in service, pulling ploughs, as well as donkeys and little ponies hauling rice carts. In some towns they are set to work pulling carriages—some of these even have stylish red velvet seats. In some places there are rickshaws, of course.

When all else fails, foot power is employed and there is never a shortage of people walking on the roads, often carrying heavy loads, some almost covered by rice sheaves, a mountain of bamboo or baskets tied together and rising high above their heads like cane parachutes.

One day we squeeze another person into our vehicle. A young woman has been waiting for a bus for four days. The public transport system in outlying areas is erratic at best and often non-existent, which explains why people wanting a lift continually pester us along the route. Although we see trucks often enough, their open trays are loaded beyond the limit with people standing and waving to us.

Trains in China are another thing altogether. They are smooth, efficient, they run on time and you get to meet the locals. Li, our guide in Turpan, in north-east China, is responsible for helping us catch the train to Dunhuang, further along the Silk Road. His English is quite good although sometimes his accent gives us something to chew over. As he readies us for the train's arrival, he is adamant that we should give our tickets to the *witches* once we have boarded.

We are not aware of any occult crews on Chinese trains, but as this is our first experience of using them, we are prepared for anything. The train arrives about ten minutes early and Li helps us on with our luggage. I am looking for the tall conical hat of our witch, but none appears. A few minutes later however, a lady conductor—whose office is right next door to our cabin—appears and, as we hand across our tickets, we realise that she is indeed the *witches* or waitress for this carriage.

We have a four-berth cabin and our companions are two men. The one with the dark complexion and fine features of the Uigyar people, wearing a traditional round cap, takes the top. He doesn't speak, is fairly restless and coughs most of the night. The other, a Han Chinese I guess, takes the bottom bunk. He smiles and we show him some pictures on the laptop, but he too wants an early night it seems or maybe he's not into holiday pics and climbs into bed fairly soon after we leave the station.

The carriage is compact and we just manage to fit in all our luggage, jig-sawing it away, stashing some things under the bed, others into the overhead cavity that extends across the corridor, but even so I end up sleeping with the tripod under my pillow. We are comforted to note that the locks on the door are very secure.

We are quite impressed with the standard of this train. It is very clean, there is a communal bathroom nearby and a *sit down* toilet at the end of our carriage. The beds appear quite comfortable, with an eiderdown, a pillow and towel—plenty for a few hours. There's even a little string mesh rack above the bed for glasses and incidentals. To reach the top bunk, however, you have to use very small steps and haul yourself up, which is why I have called on my gender and age (okay, and my size and lack of fitness) to secure the lower berth.

Two large thermoses of hot water are provided in the cabin so, before he turns in, the Chinese man uses some to prepare himself a supper of instant noodles.

We wake the next morning to see the Nullarbor outside—well that's what it looks like—and we are speeding across a flat plate of land complete with silver tufts of saltbush, the horizon a distant row of blue hills. Later we learn that we have travelled over 800 kilometres overnight and crossed the Gobi desert—at least a corner of it. Although we feel like mighty explorers, I doubt there is a wimpier way to cross a desert.

The Chinese man unearths the thermos again and makes another pot of noodles. It appears the *witches* won't bring us any breakfast and indeed they don't have time to as, in a few more minutes, we are lunging into Dunhuang and begin the process of un-stowing all our bags and belongings.

Just days later we board another train, this time from Tianshui to X'ian. This one is a daytime trip and I am glad, as we can see where we are going. There is a 'Western' toilet in this train too, but the door is locked. Eventually, when I can stand it no longer and using my best Chinese Qing (please), I mime my desire for the male *witch* to unlock the door for me by making key-turning gestures. Amazingly, he understands me and does. There is a sign on it that states, 'No occupying when stabling', so I am careful to remember that as well as noting the one inside, which admonishes users to 'please flush closet pot'.

筷子

At stations along the way we salivate over trolleys of food being sold on the platform by attendants in blue-trimmed white jackets and white peaked caps. One cart has lychees and mangoes, carefully wrapped apples and plums. Another sells hot dishes: satays, round onion breads, hard-boiled eggs, fried chicken and noodles. We want to go out and buy some, but the *witch* says no.

Whatever you might say about Chinese town planning and urban architecture—which if anything tends to be featureless, bland, purely functional and uninspiring (read boring)—you have to hand it to them with their engineering. Outside of Tianshui the railway swoops through mountains and over valleys beside the wide riverbed of the Yellow River, believed to be the cradle of Chinese civilisation. Huge viaducts (I have misty pictures taken at speed to prove it) stride for kilometres on massive pylons and when you tire of that the line plunges into a tunnel through a mountain, emerging on the other side to the same thing again. I guess we shouldn't be surprised at this expertise. After all, today's Chinese are simply following a proud tradition that kicked off centuries ago with one of the world's all-time most ambitious building projects, the Great Wall.

筷
子

# 14. UNPLEASANTRIES

*Burn a forest to farm and drain a pond to fish.*

**3000-year-old Chinese saying—showing respect for the environment**

This chapter had to happen sooner or later. While China is a magnificent country and its people are largely friendly, sociable and hospitable, there is a dark side to the place, just as there is everywhere. Rather than pepper this book with the disturbing, the ugly, the dangerous and the messy, I thought it best to collect them together here. That way, if you are a die-hard Pollyanna, have a weak stomach or simply don't want to know, you can quickly flick through to the next chapter. You have been warned.

We stop one morning in a small town somewhere along the Silk Road. Right now I can't remember the name—I think I may have subconsciously blotted it out—which is just as well. It is one of those mandatory breaks, toilets for me, pics for Gordon and a smoke for the driver who has pulled over near a hotel with a white-tiled front and red and gold banners outside, identical to many all over the country.

Of course, my motto is 'if in doubt go shopping' so, as we have been given a few minutes more, we wander along the nearest street. The first

筷子

shop displays fur-lined caps and some mats made from animal pelts. I feel uncomfortable with those so move on to the next shop and the next and the next, only to discover that each one specialises in furs of some sort: coats, caps, mats, wall hangings, scarves and—while fur is not my thing these are even more gross.

Entire Arctic fox pelts, heads intact, hang by the dozen alongside the more common ginger ones, fashioned so they can be artlessly thrown around the shoulders like a stole. Beside them lies a larger animal, a wolf maybe, a dark band down its golden back and next to that what looks like a dozen cat skins, sewn together to make a rug, perhaps. Worse still there are furs and skins from tiger, ocelot, leopard, bear and other rare and endangered species, some of which I do not even recognise, so beautiful and so precious and the price tags reflect this.

I feel sick to my stomach and look more closely. With a surge of hope I think that maybe they are fakes, dyed to look like mink and ermine or a clever nylon reproduction printed to resemble tiger. Rabbit even would be preferable, but they are not. Checking on the Internet on our return, I discover that China is regarded as the world's largest exporter of fur clothing and the biggest fur trade production and processing base in the world. Fur from China is sold throughout the EU, accounting for sales there alone of around US$4.525 million (A$6.054 million). According to one report, the British Fur Trade Association alone turns over around £500 million (A$1178 million) a year as the world's largest buyer of pelts. Many of the animals for the fur trade are raised in captivity—does this make it any better? I don't think so. I read one account of how these creatures are brutally handled and slaughtered and, trust me, you don't want to know what that means.

It is a long street and the dozen or so shops we have already passed are stuffed with these products and, as far as we can see, it seems the same further along. In shop windows across the street are similar displays. Is the whole town a vast horrific slaughterhouse for these poor creatures?

筷
子

Revolted and sad we trudge back to our van without even taking a photograph. With no power to stop or report what is quite obviously a legal and open trade in these fine creatures we just want to shake off the memory and get away as fast as we can.

We had seen similar things earlier in a market far away in Kashgar. There we had gaped in disbelief—our first exposure to this—at round fur caps, coats and fur-trimmed jackets. It was cold there and an ideal place to sell these winter clothes. Someone, seeing us transfixed in horror, but interpreting it as interest tried to sell us something.

'You like?'

We shuddered. 'No, and anyway our country will not allow us to bring these things back.'

'Which country you from?'

'Australia.'

'Last week we had big group from Australia,' he boasted, 'They buy many things.'

I truly hope that was just a salesman telling lies in the hope of making a deal.

Then there are the cruel and unusual punishments our guides tell us about. Most don't bear repeating and, even as they tell us, I have to suppress an urge to plug my ears and loudly chant, 'Nah-nah, na-naaah-naaah!'

Many of these atrocities, of course, happened centuries ago and have no doubt gained in gruesomeness in their repeated retellings. Truth or not, they often seem to involve some hapless concubine who somehow fell out of favour with the Emperor and was mutilated and imprisoned in some way—massive porcelain jars seemed a favourite—yet kept alive to suffer.

On our first visit to the hutong in Beijing we dawdle along the shopping street, not really shopping, just looking at the various things for sale. One gallery has a mixed range of goods for sale, but I am distracted by a repeated banging noise near my feet. I look down and see a black crow imprisoned in a birdcage so small it can scarcely move. It is leaping from

筷子

its perch and ineffectively pecking the bar above it: leap-peck, leap-peck, leap-peck like a heartbeat, which is the noise I heard. It is a tragic sight. Already its beak is showing the effects of this constant and ineffective beating and I beg the guide to ask the owner why this poor thing is allowed to be here like this.

'He says he has black bird for sale inside,' she reports back, 'and people say it is a crow, so he has this crow to show them that it is not.'

I long to open that cage, but instead I bend down and speak softly to the bird. At home we have birds that come to our deck and I talk to them. I know we make a connection. As I croon to it, the poor thing calms and stops its interminable bids for escape for a moment.

I wish I could say I paid the man to let the creature go, but I didn't, knowing it (or one like it) would only have been recaptured as soon as I turned my back. I slept badly that night and even as we travelled the country the sight of any crow flying free made me feel sick. When we returned to the *hutong* at the end of our trip however, the shop was closed and there was no sign of the crow.

In another place, Gordon was dining alone at a rather upmarket restaurant in a rural city. The waiter, seeing he was clearly a visitor, hurried up.

'You like? We have good dishes.' He was clearly excited at what he was about to offer. 'We have bear—very spe-shul.'

Scarcely believing his hearing, Gordon raised his eyebrows in question. A Chinese man at the next table, hearing the exchange, lifted his head and nodded.

'Yes, very good. I am eating tiger myself,' and he grinned his satisfied approval. 'I come here often. There are many exotic meats and I eat them all,' he said and leered. 'It is good for my virility.'

While cruelty to animals and their exploitation is one thing, humans are at risk too. During the 122-kilometre trip from Urumchi to Heavenly Lake—a place that truly lives up to its name—we travel many kilometres through a gloomy belt of orange fog, slumped over the land in a heavy, apparently toxic, layer. Despite the very obvious smokestacks and shining tanks of heavy industry located close to the road in several places our guide puts another spin on it.

'The people who live here burn coke in their kitchen stoves,' he assures us. 'They make lots of smoke.'

He argues that, because of the high mountains around, the pollution is trapped. There certainly is smoke, but the forest of apartment blocks have no chimneys that we can see and somehow we doubt that the residents would have access to enough coal to create such environmental havoc.

One of the factories manufactures car parts and we are told that many major companies have entered into joint ventures with China to produce vehicles. The night before we enjoyed wine produced as a joint venture with France and we applaud this move for more financially secure countries to assist the diligent and ambitious Chinese.

Near Dali, in the south-west Yunnan province, we see many factories too, a cigarette factory in the tobacco growing area is a no-brainer of course, but another, a mineral factory, disturbs us. Here there appear to be no OH&S (occupational health and safety) principles in place at all. The men manning the wheelbarrows and chutes are covered with the stuff, looking like bronze statues somehow brought to life. Later that same day, at a limestone crushing plant, the workers caked in dust resemble those white figures you see in museum displays where clothes and bodies are frosted entirely white. While they present a weird and surreal sight, it is even more frightening to think what their lungs must look like!

A day or so earlier, after our stay in Lijiang, we bumped our way through to a road that ran alongside the mighty Yangtse River, the world's third longest river at over 6000 kilometres long. At this point it was a wide and ponderous expanse of water, the colour of custard. There were several huge factories along the way, located right on the riverbank, obviously for ease of transport of their raw material, but we sensed another, more sinister, reason.

We stopped to watch the effluent from a paper and wood-chipping mill pouring into the water. As we travelled downriver the tide of white scum stayed with us for many kilometres. Above it the sky was choked with smoke, the sun a dim disc beyond. Other industries dealt with mineral sands and, when we reached those, most of the dull blue trucks we passed, belching nauseating bursts of black smoke over us, carried blue metal and we were glad to be past them as soon as possible.

China's huge cities have their own pollution problems to deal with. The morning we land at Chengdu we descend from sunshine at 39 000 feet into a bowl of white goo, which covers the city and its 12 million people, who are no doubt choking to death. The air is so thick we feel we could cut it. It is supposed to be noted for its hibiscus and there is a famous zoo (poor animals!) especially devoted to a panda-breeding program. You have to wonder how they feel about it.

A young man called Charlie—with three facial hairs and cigarette breath—escorts us saying it is a bad day for pollution for Chengdu. Hmm! Trying to be charitable and hoping we have simply caught the place on a bad day, I ask another local, 'Is it always like this?'

'No,' he replies, 'it is always like this.'

Not only the rivers and cities are at risk, China's Maritime Safety

Administration recently stated that the country's economic boost has resulted in an increase of shipping and this, coupled with a lack of adequate environmental laws, means the seas are experiencing 'unprecedented levels of pollution', while huge oil spills threaten the coasts and adjoining inland areas.

So there, it's over now. I've finished my sad little collection of anecdotes and it would be not so bad if these were all. In a country of well over a billion people, scattered over millions of square kilometres of countryside cut by huge rivers and in massive cities, where sunlight rarely penetrates, there has to be much more. China is aware of all these 'unpleasantries' as well as thousands of others. It just needs to figure out a way of dealing with them.

*Once was a snow leapord*

## 15. BOOTS, BUDDHAS AND HEAVENLY HORNS

*It's better to light a candle than to curse the darkness.*

**Chinese proverb**

Quing!

The maroon-robed monk rattles his beads impatiently. He's looking straight at us and saying 'please!' but in rather un-monk-like exasperation. He wants us to quit taking photos and follow him on the Labrung Lamasery tour. He has a heavy morning ahead, involving deafening mournful horn music followed by kicking off his knee-high felt boots and filing into the monastery with a few hundred fellow monks for a lengthy ceremony. Seems he wants to get on with it.

Despite his grim look, I am delighted because I understand him. Qing (pronounced 'ching' and only to be used at the beginning of a sentence) is one of four Mandarin words I have mastered along the Silk Road. The others (hello and thank you) have been worn threadbare, but not as much as bu hsehhsieh (pronounced 'boo shay shay' and meaning no, thank you) said with firmness on many occasions in response to offers of everything from wristwatches to postcards and myriad other flim-flam.

I think I may have words or the inflection wrong because I hear people parroting it and giggling when I think I've said it just right. Chinese is such a tonal language that a different up or down emphasis can change some words catastrophically. Every guide tells us the several meanings of 'ma' which, depending on the tone you use, can mean mother, horse or hemp and can be used as a curse.

We are in Little Tibet, Xiahe in Ganzhou province, at an altitude of 3000 metres where it's a surprise to find an authentic lamasery (lama's monastery), and one of the largest in the country, so far from Tibet. Yet a glance at the map and I see that—on the eastern extremity of the Tibetan plateau—this settlement is the last of a receding tide. Here, they refer to the place we call Tibet as West Tibet.

'The lamasery was established in 1390,' our guide says. He has taken the name of Steed, because he likes horses and he feels it is a strong name. 'It took 300 years to develop into the largest yellow-hat seat in the country.'

He tells us there are around 1400 lamas and monks based here and, when I wander through the town later in the day, they are everywhere, lounging at tables, strolling with friends, chatting on their mobiles or sitting in the sun.

A truck goes past with maybe thirty young monks standing in the back, squealing and hooting like adolescent boys would anywhere. I learn that they only have classes in the morning, but the rest of the day is their own. I wonder if they get bored.

'Be at the courtyard before ten-thirty,' Steed tells us.

So we are, but the activities have already begun at the lamasery with a few mournful notes blown through a conch shell from the top corners of the main building. Monks have been assembling here for half an hour, wriggling into position on the steep flight of steps at the front.

The onlookers are mainly locals, Tibetan by appearance and wearing thick sheepskin-lined coats and cloaks that I suspect cover many other layers, tied at the waist by wide strips of fabric. One woman's long dark

筷
子

hair is braided into a hundred or so tiny plaits. All of these people have a sense of anticipation about them.

The lamasery itself seems a little faded, the rose pink paint, higher up, peeling and the white below scuffed and smudged by the hundreds of hands that must touch the wall each day. The gold ridgepole and ornaments on the tiled roof glitter proudly in the sunlight, however, and the intricately patterned curtains and banners flutter in the light breeze. Under the eaves, blue, green and orange highlight the fine carving detail and I wish I had more time to learn their meaning.

If colour means anything, Buddhism is a happy religion. The dimmest and most obscure temples glow with bright, primary hues and even the tiniest tapestries and wall hangings are luminous. Silver and gold sparkle as accents and there are rainbow ribbons, bows and baubles, pompoms and tassels, fringes and pleats, braids and embroidery that carry it into a psychedelic third dimension. Buddhism begets busy decor, crammed with flamboyant decoration.

By contrast the monks' clothing is austere: a heavy blanket-like cape slung around their shoulders over a simple sashed robe. I notice as they line up in the sunshine on the steps that the maroon I have always talked about, when describing their outfits, actually ranges from a dark blood colour through rusty red to hot pink.

A huge stone burner, squatting like a massive pizza oven in a far corner of the courtyard, has been lit for some time and the sweet-acrid smell from the blue smoke of a particular type of fragrant pine hangs like a prayer around us. This is obviously a special ceremony as the monks are all wearing magnificent, stiff, creamy felt headdresses that rise high in the front and fit snugly over their short-cropped hair. A thick band of woollen fleece extends from the back at the nape of their necks to the tip of the peak, curving beyond like a comma. It has something of the look of a high-church Mohawk about it. While most wear these with respect and dignity, a few show a fearless streak of independence, setting them jauntily

筷子

askew. Some much younger novices, just children, arrive later, playing up to the older monks, playfully whacking them with their head-dresses, climbing on them and generally making a nuisance of themselves, like kids anywhere.

I covet the boots most. Finally, with no sense of rush or pressure, the steps are filled and then slowly taking off their long boots and leaving them where they fall, the monks rise and stroll barefoot into the monastery. Now I can see that these boots are made from black felt—warm as toast I would imagine on a cold Tibetan morning—and trimmed at the top with red binding, the soles sensibly thick rubber, ideal for walking around the stony lamasery grounds.

It is impossible to know what this service is about or understand its relative importance in the scheme of lamasery life, but I sneak up to the doorway regardless to see what is going on inside. Other tourists do too and no one seems to mind for a while, until we are politely shuffled off.

Inside, in the dim interior, the monks are all seated on mats. There is one, obviously some dignitary, dressed in a heavy robe, pleated at the shoulders with a panel at the back stiff with jewels and metals glowing in the gloom. There is chanting, too—a constant baritone hum.

Now here is the bit I don't understand. People who obviously want to make a donation to the monks are throwing wads of money, balled up, through the open door. The monks catch these and add them to their piles. Later I see them outside in little groups, counting and comparing.

A low sound like a wind—a combination of mumbled prayers, soft hand claps, chanting and the handling of money and beads—comes from inside. As the service goes on for some time, the monks I can see near the edge of the temple seem eager to be going, playing with their hands, chatting with each other, even flicking the ends of the back panel of the head lama's robe as he passes.

Soon some are instructed to bring the yak butter tea, which they collect from the kitchen next door, dispensing it to those still inside from

筷子

large spouted brass jugs with a handle on each side to make carrying them easier. There is a lot of movement until finally, a few at a time and with little pomp, the monks come out of the temple, somehow find their own boots from the mass of discarded ones on the steps, then stand around in groups, chatting and swapping stories. It could have been a sunny morning after mass or morning service back home, but for the robes.

*Yak butter tea*

筷子

No one knows how many Buddhists there are in China. Some estimate there are 102 million adherents. While monks have had a tense and terrible time for many years, even until quite recently, the powers that be now seem to have softened and are even working to rebuild monasteries that were damaged or destroyed by previous administrations.

As we travel the Silk Road, Buddhas are everywhere and I admit that on some days (no disrespect meant here) I feel completely Buddha-ed out. The Bezeklik Thousand Buddha Caves, 45km northeast of Turpan give us reason to consider things differently.

'These ancient frescoes,' the guide on duty tells us, 'were plundered by German scientists in the early twentieth century.'

She means archaeologists, but the result is the same. It's hard to imagine people, especially professional researchers, removing this priceless art of deep religious significance so that it could be displayed in German museums. Worse was to come.

'Many of these stolen frescoes were later destroyed in bombing during World War II.'

Photographs, taken prior to their theft, are propped outside the grottoes, but it is not the same.

The next day, hundreds of kilometres west at the Mogao grottoes of Dunhuang, we see frescoes that escaped the adhesives used to remove the Bezeklik ones and also the devastation of the Cultural Revolution. The caves are now World Heritage listed.

One grotto certainly has the 'wow factor' we feel. Here a massive 35.5-metre-high Buddha in a yellow robe has been carved from the rock. He holds his huge right hand up, like a stop signal, while the left is cupped, but so tall is it that we find it impossible to clearly see his features in perspective. They are foreshortened, doll-like in the distance. Nearby is a reclining Buddha, sixteen metres long and looking very comfortable, depicted in Nirvana surrounded by his disciples. Of course we expect to find Buddhas here. Buddhism arrived in China from India, maybe as early

筷子

as the third century BC, as believers travelled along with the riches from central Asia and beyond.

We boarded a boat to cross a lake—really the Liujiaxia Dam—some distance from Lan Zhou to reach Binglingsi and its Thousand Buddha caves, one of China's premier religious sites. While the myriad Buddhas—painted on walls, carved and hidden in grottoes and caves, ranging from plain clay and doll-sized, to massive and gilded—are awesome, the 27-metre-high Buddha carved into the rock face overlooking the river takes our breath away. Although created in the eighth century, a pavilion was later built to cover and protect this. It was only during a war in the eighteenth century when this was burnt away that the Buddha was rediscovered.

For 20 yuan each we take a short ride in a green open-topped jeep further up the river valley. Here, among mountains that rise like daggers into the clear sky, we are introduced to a gentle monk who shows us around his simple temple and the spotless compound where the rest of the order of monks live. He speaks very fast and totally unintelligible English, so we nod a lot and he smiles a lot. He must sense our liking for him, however, and admiration for his way of life because, as we leave, he presses a complexly folded triangle of paper into my hand.

'It's a prayer,' our guide translates. 'He is blessing you.'

Years before, in Tibetan country, near Zhongdiang we enter through extremely beautiful and brightly painted doors to steps that take us up to a lamasery. We rest often as it is high here and there must be 100 steps in all. Eventually we arrive at the top and enter the huge main hall. It's pitch dark, but we use torches until our eyes become accustomed to the feeble light from the coconut butter lamps.

'This monastery was completely wrecked during the cultural revolution,' our guide says, 'they have been seventeen years trying to fix it up. They have some very old statues of Buddha, lamas and gods and a picture of the Panchen Lama: the little lost one.'

筷
子

The lamasery is bare except for prayer rugs on small low shelves and huge hanging coloured cloths, yet there is a simple beauty to it.

We climb even more stairs to meet the head lama, but discover that he moonlights as a doctor and has been called out on a house call. The view from the rooftop looking back over Zhongdiang is impressive anyway, so we linger. A young monk—a twelve-year-old lad seated on the floor nearby—chants his lessons at a tiny table, so totally engrossed in his studies he hardly notices us. With permission we take his picture and that of an older monk sitting in front of the window who wants to share some yellowed yak cheese with us. Then gender discrimination takes over and the men in our group are invited to look in the kitchen, but we women are not. It was very plain anyway, the guys say on their return, possibly to make us feel better.

Near Lijiang—at the temple where we saw the ancient fir tree that had been split in half by lightning—we find a mix of sub-faiths: Pai Shai, Buddhist with Tibetan, Pai and Naxi and, in the middle of the roof, a Tibetan character meaning brightness.

'All the columns here were man-made and the frescoes in the lama temple are 600 years old,' we are told by the custodian through our interpreter. 'There are more than 525 frescoes and it took artists 200 years to finish them all.'

Sadly, they are neglected now, protected only by a black curtain on a wire and a chain in a couple of places. They have enormous religious significance and many stories are connected with them. The eyes were originally made of gold and gems, but these were all stolen during the Cultural Revolution. Domba means 'wise men' and they talk about Domba scriptures, which are either here or once were.

At another place, deeper in Tibet, our leader wants us to see what he calls the sandalwood monastery. One of the other vehicles is well ahead of us (could the photographers in our car be to blame?). When we catch up with them at the next town we find that they have been accosted by

筷子

the military police and have only just avoided being forced to go to the police station.

They resisted, fortunately, and when we turn up we have to hand over our passports for checking too. We wait about an hour before we are informed that we cannot see the monastery anyway. We wonder if something happened at or to the monastery, but all we can do is hope that all is well and look at it from across the valley.

Finally, we reach Lhasa, the Forbidden City, and are drawn like a magnet to its icon, the towering maroon and white Potala Palace—bereft of its traditional master, the exiled Dalai Lama—aloof and perhaps more stunning when seen from a distance. We spend a couple of hours here captivated by the interiors, clambering up stairs, enjoying the space and relative calm, as well as the views across the city. Its prominent position means that wherever you are, in Lhasa there is usually a corner visible and it stands a solid reminder, despite the red and yellow flag flying over it, that Tibetan culture survives.

For many tourists the Potala is the symbol of Tibet, but it is not a monastery or temple so we follow the crowds, some slowly prostrating themselves and rising over and over, sliding their threadbare mat or piece of cardboard forward each time, inching their way to a goal they may have dreamed of reaching for their entire lives. They come in all shapes and sizes, these worshippers at Johkang, the main temple in the city. I am also impressed by how many are quite young.

Here tall stone furnaces burn branches that give off the scent that is the signature of temples throughout China. I call it holy smoke, but gasp when I pass one and swallow a lungful. I make a mental note to ask if I am now somehow purified.

The place is full of blue, yellow, white, green and red prayer flags printed with Tibetan script. There are drum-shaped brass prayer wheels, strategically located so people can give them a spin as they pass and send their prayers off with a flourish. We have arrived at the Jokhang on an auspicious day we learn—the thirtieth day of the eighth month—and so the crush to get in is even greater than usual.

'Eight, fifteen and thirty have auspicious meaning for visiting pilgrims,' the guide, an older man with a wispy beard tells us. 'Today it is doubly so.'

Everywhere we see people lighting butter lamps with ghee they have bought outside. They press hard together, clinging to each other's shoulders, the eagerness they feel at finally entering this holy place evident on their faces. Some have travelled many kilometres—we may have passed some of them crammed onto the back of open 'buses' or even a few coming the hardest way, prostrating themselves.

There are Khampas, with their brilliant red headdresses, women carrying babies on their backs and children with a black smudge on their faces to protect them on their first visit, I am told. Inside I can just glimpse a red column draped with fabric, so we know we are nearly there. There must be thousands of people I figure and, while hundreds are pressing in, an equal number, who have finished, are fighting to leave creating a sort of religious gridlock.

Finally, we are in front of the altar. I see prayer mats, a lady with turquoise in her black hair holding a silver lamp, others lighting butter lamps with great concentration and a number of side rooms, called chapels, with chain screens. In one a nun is praying and, when she looks up and sees us, she wishes us all a long life. The crowd is humming *omani padani om* and it swells to fill the space like a great organ tone.

I begin to feel a little claustrophobic. The doors are low and there's a confusing range of different statues, including one said to have 1000 arms. We move clockwise as we must, out of respect as well as self-preservation. To go another way would result in anger at the least, but possibly trampling on such a busy day.

As we go upstairs a brass bell rings and we move towards a brightly lit space. A man prostrates himself at my feet, people are praying all around me and there is a sense of devout wonder. Nearby an old woman reaches out and hits a bell with her walking stick. Then we are at the most holy place where the curtains are made from heavy links of iron and young monks direct the way.

The stairs are slippery with spilt butter and wax from the lamps. The heat is stifling. I notice some pilgrims paying homage by putting their heads down on scarves around the throne, which up this close I can also see is all real: solid silver, genuine turquoise, coral, amber and gold. This place is worth a fortune.

Nearby a man with a thermos is walking and chanting and it is then that I really notice the brightly painted murals. Every exposed area is carved, painted and decorated, even the ceiling. Ranks of maroon-robed, haloed Buddhas gaze down, as if in heaven, on the thousands who come here. On another wall a particularly agitated navy-blue god stamps on someone. He has skulls decorating his hairline and little heads peep out from around his body.

'You can take away a people's possessions, lands and rights,' says a voice near my ear, 'but you can't take away what is in their hearts and heads. Once there were 20 000 monks in the various monasteries in Lhasa.' It is our guide.

'Well, I think,' says Marjorie from our group who has heard him, 'that the Chinese flag flying over the monasteries is like seeing a swastika over a synagogue.'

One of the more amazing things we see—although it may just be my interest in cooking—are some yak butter sculptures on the third level. They are here to underline the impermanence of everything, but they appear more like pretty confections, lightly pastel tinted with bright red highlights. They would look equally at home in a patisserie back in Australia.

Finally we make it to the rooftop where we can look down on the two large effigies in the main area. One seems disapproving, the other slightly

筷子

sleepy. There is a couch that the Dalai Lama once sat on and six hangings stitched with devoted and intricate detail.

Below we can see makeshift stalls selling drinks and biscuits—pilgrim sustenance I guess—and out of the smoky view rise forests of branches with prayer flags on them and a press of people, still hanging on to each other.

Huge kilns burn incense, juniper and tsampa. People throw in hand-fuls and the smoke belches out, amber and grey. It's a busy place down there with people prostrating themselves. There's a swishing noise as they each move their cardboard mats forward, the percussion against the low vocal chant, Om, Om, Om.

From the roof we can see across to the Potala Palace and we sight it again from the roof of the Yak Hotel, where we are staying, fittingly framed by prayer flags.

We leave Lhasa early one morning for Shigatse, the seat of the Panchen Lama, 220 km south-west of Lhasa. Someone has heard that there is to be a special monks' musical festival at the monastery that day.

When we arrive a large crowd is already here and we realise that this is something very big, scarcely able to believe our visit has coincided with it. As if we are truly important we are ushered to special seats right at the front of the large open space as big as a playing field and given tea and little nibbles while we wait for things to begin.

Across on the other side the monks sit in their maroon robes, magnif-icent in tall golden headdresses that curve over their heads like giant apostrophes. Among them are child novices, wriggling around and no doubt wishing they could go and play. One, a serious and very young child, sits close to the head of the temple and I ask why he is there. I am told that perhaps he has been chosen to become a holy man one day.

The music begins almost as soon as we are seated. A man in a richly quilted and embroidered outfit dances towards us. An effigy tops his broad-brimmed hat and I am at a loss to know if he represents good or evil.

筷子

The morning is filled with colour and movement. Monks wearing red, gold and purple scarves parade past swinging censers. Others follow, wearing massive papier-mâché animal heads, then performers of all sorts, clad in the brightest, shiniest, most ornate outfits. A masked troupe of performers dance together and what must be clowns make even the monks burst into smiles. My eyes hurt with the colour and wealth of sensory input.

For me, the real star turn of this kaleidoscopic day comes at the end when several monks stand and take up enormous brass horns—at least three metres long, so long they need to rest the ends on the ground to play them—and begin a mournful barping fanfare, the deafening two-note range low and visceral. This groaning fills the space with sounds of agony and there is no room left in our heads, in the temple grounds or in the universe it seems for anything other than this.

It goes on and on ... then stops. Just like that. While our ears still sting with the sudden silence those children, the young novices, bound up immediately, followed more slowly by the monks, and disappear off-stage.

Next day we visit the Tashilhungpo monastery, built in 1447. It is very large and we visit several chapels as well as the chanting hall. One is very new and beautiful with the silk banners (I call them neckties) glowing in the low light, but suddenly it seems such a waste that the stooped and obviously poor pilgrims with hardly two yuan to rub together, who we see slowly circling the Buddhas and sacred relics, must contribute to these places that are dripping with gold. That's religion, anywhere in the world, I guess. The counter-argument is that these beautiful places raise people's minds to the heavenly. Some say the government is rebuilding them to make a show of allowing religion to flourish now. Others say they skim off the offerings. It is very hard to get a true picture, if indeed there is one.

There are dozens of thin yellow dogs outside in the courtyards and the word is that they can be quite dangerous, but this particular day they all seem yelped-out after a hard night of barking and most are asleep, sprawled in the sun on the cobblestones. Some believe that these temple dogs are the reincarnation of lazy monks who failed to learn their lessons properly. This sounds more like a cautionary tale to me, one devised to keep the young guys over their books.

Whatever the case, it hardly matters to me whether it's a potentially rabid dog or a reincarnated monk that's nipping at my ankles. Although we have taken the precaution of having rabies injections before leaving Australia, I take the safe option and align myself with the stick and tripod-bearing members of our group

筷子

# 16. MA DONG SHI, LET'S GO SHOPPING!

*When you have only two pennies left in the world,*
*buy a loaf of bread with one and a lily with the other.*
**Chinese Proverb**

The cloud of dust in the valley is a clue. Our driver jabbers to the guide and he nods, so we drive down and park. Someone struggles past. At least I presume there is a person under that massive basket of scarlet chillies, curved like tiny red fingers. A donkey, loaded up with two bamboo panniers stuffed with herbs and vegetables, stands waiting, seemingly lost in thought.

Nearby a Bai woman—I recognise the clothing from a cultural display we have seen the day before—in a red waistcoat and red, yellow and blue embroidered headdress is sorting out things for her stall. She has added a cream straw hat on top of her traditional headpiece, giving her an oddly South American look.

We realise now why there was so much dust. Here, there are hundreds of horses and donkeys, all pack animals, quiet now and relaxing while their masters sell whatever they have brought before purchasing more to take away again.

Not being in the market for a crate of melons or a sackful of chillies, the pressure on me to buy is reduced, so I relax and wander around. The retail section of the market is selling those same wide-brimmed straw hats and doing a brisk trade, for the sun is scorching. There is a good line of noodle soups going too for this sort of trading is hungry work.

I love markets and my need for retail therapy is well looked after in China as markets pop up in almost every town, all day, any day and—to my never-ending delight and Gordon's mystification—even at night. In fact a night market is a wonderful thing, time to unwind and relax as the day cools, a chance to grab a bit of local food for dinner and swap smiles, if not conversation, with the stall-holders.

Markets, bazaars, stalls, souks, pavement shops or hawker's baskets, call them what you like, they all spell the same thing. A slice of the action, a few great deals and a chance to learn how the locals do it. Just follow the crowds. Ask the locals. Go with an open mind and wallet, for you will be tempted to buy. Nothing surer!

The word 'bazaar' was once 'wazar' in ancient Eastern texts. Later, this Farsi word was introduced into other languages, so now we have bazaar in English, *bazar* in French, Portuguese, Turkish and Indian, *pasar* in Malay and Indonesian and *pazar* and *vazar* in Polish. No doubt it came along for the ride with the earliest traders between East and West, possibly via the Silk Road when it was one long bazaar itself.

The Chinese are great entrepreneurs, a nation of business people and there is nothing they love more than to close a deal. As I have admitted I love to shop so it's a good mix. An essential phrase to learn, early on, is *Ma Dong Shi*, which translates as 'let's go shopping', although in ancient times it meant 'let's go to the East (or West) market'.

Made in China: I've picked those labels off souvenir koalas, yet when people travel they have to bring something back for those at home who missed out on the fun of the trip. It is not always necessary to seek out a market, sometimes it comes to us.

筷子

One morning, scarcely awake somewhere in Tibet, I rub the sleep out of my eyes to see a young woman, her hands plunged deep into the folds of her grubby cloak, watching us. This is not unusual, but like any good salesperson the moment she catches my eye, she withdraws a crude dagger, its handle covered with beaten silver that has been fashioned in places to hold knobs of turquoise and coral. I take a closer look, which encourages her, and see that they are real, but I don't want a knife.

Once I have made that clear, she tosses back a dark plait and retrieves something else. This time it is a strange-looking leather case, very small which, when she opens, I see contains needles. Now this would be a prized possession for a nomadic person, a way to keep at hand the tools to make many garments. The leather is dyed pink with a green decoration, tiny pieces snipped out to create a relief texture and I can only imagine how hard it must have been for wind-chapped fingers to punch the stitching through the stiff hide, but it is neat and the inside has been lined with something soft. There is another smaller thing attached to it and I see that, if I pull a leather thong, it opens and reveals a space just right for a thimble.

It is unique and I haggle half-heartedly—I have already fallen for her guileless face and don't have the desire to beat the price down too much—paying fifty yuan. I relent and buy the dagger as well. It will do for a gift. Just as she is turning to leave I have a thought, opening the needle case.

'Here,' I say, 'keep these. I have plenty more at home.'

Of course she doesn't understand the words, but she takes them gratefully.

Back home in Australia the needle case hangs on my wall, but it was months before it lost the smell of the peat fires from the tent where it was made and I was almost sorry when it did.

Markets are the same the world over. There is always the absolute rubbish that is poorly made, ugly, overpriced and a total waste of space.

Fifty percent of tourist purchases belong to this category. What is more, these items appear over and over again. At markets throughout China each stall may display a cloned range of glass globes, plastic back scratchers, clay teapots, 'antique' books, rings set with bits of rock and glass, enamel bracelets that break the first day, stone vases and lacquer-look chopsticks. They are arranged generally without any consideration of style, placement or appeal.

Then there are the other things and, because I know that if you have read this far you must love shopping too, here is a basketful of some things I saw and bought, some I wish I had and some I am glad I didn't.

In Shigatse, beyond Lhasa, I visit a row of canopied stalls in a dusty street. We buy a knife then stand in amazement when someone points out that there are skulls for sale. Lama's skulls they say. I pass on those.

There is a meat market nearby too with carcasses hanging. The meat simply hacked off as requested. People buy the meat, clasp it to their clothes and keep shopping. There are also huge balls of yak butter, which I am pleased to note that, when fresh, smells fine. It is funny in the streets here to get a whiff of the butter as people pass. Yak butter tea is a huge favourite with the nomads.

Later that day we visit a carpet factory. Here, girls are working seated on cushions, creating lovely patterns on the tufted rugs in front of them. We watch as they work quickly and skilfully and there is a lot of happy laughter and chatter in the air. It is a bright room and I have no idea how they follow the pattern. It seems to be either sketched on paper well above where they are working or they must carry it in their heads.

The work is meticulous, the wool is thick and punching it through the backing must take some strength. I notice that the delicate fingers of many of the girls are nicked by this difficult work, so I fish in my bag for some bandaids I've brought on the trip. They are coloured—I'd imagined sharing them with children—but this suits the girls' artistic tastes and as I pass them around as fairly as I can, they clamour for more, showing me

筷子

even more cuts and abrasions. Of course I buy a rug too and now at home its blue and cream pattern reminds me always of those busy girls, laughing despite their sore fingertips.

In Lijiang I buy something very strange. Chinese people love to present things well and one stall has a pile of small cardboard boxes, covered in printed paper with a ribbon and plastic latch. Inside I find a small green marble roller about eight centimetres wide attached to a handle made from green plastic.

'What is this?' I mime.

Someone helps with the answer: 'It is for your skin, to massage, so you don't get old.'

With such a sales pitch of course I buy one, two actually, the second for a friend who looks at me strangely when I give it to her. I don't know whether it works or not because I have to say I haven't used it much, which might explain why there have been no appreciable results.

In many of these places, the salespeople have a complicated way with calculators, punching in an endless amount of figures, cancelling the result and putting in another set. Impossible to follow, but in the end all that matters, I guess, is 'do you want to pay this much?'

In Lhasa, after the mandatory tours of temples and palaces, I slip the leash and head for the Barkhor, the meandering maze-like market area. I feel like I have lost a few centuries too, as here I could be in the Middle Ages, surrounded by people in strange clothing: capes and cloaks, turbans and cloth caps.

There are all the accoutrements of Buddhist worship for sale here too, of course, for this area lies in the shadow of the Johkang. There are flags and banners, prayer wheels, beads and those white silky stoles presented with gifts. It's impossible to visit the temple without being tempted by the stallholders or covered in the smoke from the incense consumed by those portly stone burners at the entrance to the temple.

Some tables sell pieces of cloth and there are people conveniently set up nearby with their sewing machines. Elsewhere in a dim alley a table holds cuts of meat and, except for the oriental faces of the people, there is

a Dickensian feel to it all. I half-expect to see Fagan and his accomplices lurking behind a corner.

There are rugs and carpets too—some like the one I have already bought and had shipped home—and soft blankets and coarse coats, for it is chilly even now in autumn, and I am sure that winter at an altitude of 3700 metres will be frigid. Women pass me with felt-lined sheepskin blankets sashed around their waists already.

Most confronting of all is a framed display case of gold teeth, safely protected by glass but shining alluringly on their cottonwool backing. Just in case people don't realise what they are, a full set of white ones is laid out in the centre with a picture of a pretty woman in a hat, flashing (literally) a smile. It stands propped up amongst the rugs and presumably you pick the size you need—they all seem to be incisors—and someone in a nearby clinic/shop is no doubt on standby to install them on the spot.

Then there are the food markets. Near Lan Zhou, at a small town called Shuiquan, we smell the onions before we see them on sale in an open space beside the road. I have never seen so many green onions in my life. There are truckloads of them, their long green tops dangling limply over the sides. Men in cloth caps and mismatched suits stand around smoking as they discuss the produce.

Some take their business negotiations to a rough shelter at the side of the grounds, but most seem content to barter back and forth until they are satisfied with the deal. We stroll amongst them taking photographs, saying 'Ni hao' (hello) and marvelling at the length of some of these onions. Most stretch a metre or more, right across the tray of the popular local farm vehicle, something resembling a blue three-wheeled motor-bike, but with a long wheelbase and a utility-sized tray behind the driver's seat.

Just a couple of doors down the road I find a house set up with a few cauliflowers, cabbages and nashi pears on a table outside. When I stop to photograph them a woman emerges and eagerly poses with them, proving herself a natural performer for the camera. She knows it too and mimes that she wants me to send the picture to her.

In Urumchi—a key city on the major trade road into Kajakisthan and Russia at the beginning of our trip down the Silk Road—we visit an indoor market. Immediately a woman offers me saffron and I notice that almost every stall has it in jars decorated with purple crocus flowers.

Nearby is a mosaic of fruit and nuts in shades from grey to green to gold and brown. The owner hands me a green sultana and I feel I would be rude not to eat it. It is delicious of course, because this whole area is known for the grapes it grows, mainly for drying. The shopkeeper hands me something else, an almond that has been roasted in the shell. It is slightly cracked so I can see the browned nut inside. It is so good that I buy a bagful, as well as another one filled with those tiny dried figs I know in Australia as Iranian figs. Those bags are to last us the entire trip, standing in for the odd meal we miss when travelling.

The whole lower area of this huge place is given over to fruit, fresh

筷子

and dried. There are dried apricots with the kernel inside, dried pineapple, plums, dates, muscatels and nuts of all descriptions, fresh and beautifully presented. Upstairs, we find a sort of department store with Russian-style fur hats and nesting Russian dolls, reminding us how far into Central Asia we have come. It is a trader's caravan of exotic items: jade, pewter, bronze, carved wood, brassware, gemstones, silks, pashminas, leather coats and woollen clothing.

While China's markets are always worth a visit, so too are the shops. The only ones I am not so keen on are the Friendship Stores which are the huge, richly stocked (read expensive) government stores that are mandatory visits as part of any guided tour. I am told that the guides must include one in every day's itinerary, so I go along with the charade: them shrugging a wordless resigned apology, me determined to get it over with as swiftly as possible.

These stores usually come with some sort of industry attached, which can range from silk weaving factories or jade workshops to places making transparent stone cups, rugs or inlaid marble. It is not the quality of the goods I take issue with. What I dislike most is the shop assistant who attaches herself to me like a shadow and mirrors my movements the entire time. I have found that I can do anything: walk faster, backtrack, stand still for minutes at a time or ask them for some space. Nothing works. No doubt a commission is attached, because once they have adopted you nothing will break the relationship. Nothing. The only thing I know to do is to leave quickly.

In contrast with this sort of escorted shopping, one morning while Gordon is off taking photos, I spend a happy hour in a store in Tianshui, doing nothing more than walking the aisles, poking and prodding, picking up and turning over various items.

In some ways it is like a $2 store back home with all those smart little gadgets and things that often have 'Made in China' stamped on them. I buy some gifts for people back home and think long and hard about a

筷子

noodle press, not because it is expensive—it only costs about A$6—but because it is metal, cylindrical and strangely shaped. I don't want to spend a long time explaining it at the airport.

In the end I can't resist it, deciding to pack it deep in my suitcase. Of course it arrives without any questions asked. Now I just have to remember to use it sometime.

筷子

# 17. DYNASTY DILEMMAS AND MAJOR MINORITIES

*To forget one's ancestors is to be a brook without a source, a tree without a root.*
**Chinese proverb**

Everywhere we go in China our guides baffles us with dynasties.

'This is from the Tang dynasty,' one says as he points out a plump porcelain figure.

'This is from the Han dynasty,' advises another.

Shang, Han, Tang, Song, Qing: it's all a blur and, even as I nod knowingly, I know that I don't have a clue.

When you think of the millions of people who have lived in China throughout its long history, it's no wonder that they continue to unearth, uncover and discover so much of ancient interest. So many civilisations. So much history! For thousands of years inquisitive explorers have come here, traders have tramped back and forth across the country and marauding invaders have ram-raided the place and grabbed as much loot as they could carry off. If we are talking destruction, the powerful, local administrations in the last century were particularly harsh on the cultural heritage of China.

筷子

Somewhere I come across a list of Chinese dynasties and begin trying to memorise them. I get Tang (618–907 AD) easily enough. This one titillates me as the guide tells us that these people loved luxury, plump women and were a little risqué. I see a painting in a museum of a well-endowed empress who was said to crave lychees, eating as many as 300 in a day. I love lychees too, but they are very sweet. I wonder how she could stomach so many of them and feel sorry for her hapless courtiers who would have had to send afar for fruit to keep up with her addiction.

Then there was the Ming dynasty. I have come across porcelain from that era in museums. They ruled from 1368 to 1644 and, although this period is much more recent, it is still amazing to see the fragile, intricately decorated china from so long ago.

Ming was followed by Qing, the last dynasty before China was declared a republic and, while these first few were fairly easy to assimilate, some of the others just would not stick until I came across a chart that related them to Western history, which made much more sense for me.

So now I know that the Xia dynasty (2100–1600 BC) and the Shang dynasty (1600–1100 BC), when the earliest records begin, coincided with the times of ancient Egypt. From 3000 BC to 1600 BC most people lived along the Huang Lee (Yellow River) raising silkworms, making thread and cloth and traded these along the camel trails that led into Central Asia.

The Zhou dynasty was in power from approximately 1100 BC to 771 BC, when Assyria was at its peak. This period saw a huge growth in the understanding of medicine and was followed by the Spring and Autumn period and the Warring States, during which time the Great Wall was begun. Then came Qin, which was contemporaneous with Ancient Greece (221–207 BC).

The history of the East did not mirror the West. While the Roman empire was expanding the Han dynasty (206 BC–220 AD) brought a conflicted age of feudalism and philosophy as well as a burst of culture:

music, literature and art. Later, while the West experienced centuries of the Dark Ages, China flourished under the Three Kingdoms, Jin and Sui dynasties from 220 to 618 AD.

Tang and the Five Dynasties (618-960 AD) coincided with Charlemagne, followed by a feudal period in Europe during which the Song, Liao, Jin and Yuan dynasties from 960-1368 AD took China to new heights of invention and success with the development of block printing and movable type. Suddenly many books were available to scholars. This whole industry would have been severely hampered of course if, during the Han dynasty, paper had not been developed around 100 AD.

The Renaissance in Europe roughly matched the Ming dynasty (1368-1644), during which the Great Wall was permanently constructed. The West's Industrial Revolution occurred at the same time as the Qing dynasty (1616-1911). The remaining eras: the Republic of China (1912-1949) and the rise of the People's Republic of China in 1949 complete the tempestuous timeline of this ancient people.

Half a day's drive east of Urumchi, near Turpan, a dusty place where raisins dry in ventilated brick barns and it is so hot in summer that workers take a four-hour siesta during the heat of the day, we take a side trip to visit Jiahoe, now abandoned to the desert winds. The sign at the gate tells us poetically that it is 'located on a willow-leaf shaped plateau in the Yarnaz Valley'. We learn that its strategic position—on a low plateau that rises thirty metres over the river—was carefully selected over 2000 years ago. Today it remains, regarded as the largest, oldest and best-preserved earthen city in the world. Then it was home to 700 households, 6500 residents and 865 soldiers, its position making it an ideal defence post.

'Whoever controlled Turpan controlled the Silk Road,' Li, our guide, tells us.

On the day we visit a chill wind blows sand in our faces and we pose, for light relief, sagging against signs that say 'collapsing, keep off'. 'No

筷子

writing, no scribbling' admonishes another and I look round guiltily wondering if I should put my notebook away!

We have to squint a bit at some buildings to imagine that they were once habitable and are not simply wind-sculpted natural formations. Watch towers and sentry posts are marked, however, and the ruins of a huge Buddhist temple remind us that this place was inhabited for many hundreds of years, until around the 15th century.

The next day Li takes us further—around fifty kilometres from Turpan near the appropriately named Flaming Mountains, blazing in the early morning light—to Gaochang, another fort from the same period as Jaihoe, but now also disappearing back into the desert. At the entrance, his donkey harnessed, a brown-robed young man stands ready for us to hop on a flat cart topped with an alluring tasselled red canopy. There's even a rug to cushion the ride, but although another group chooses to use one, we decide to walk.

The carts are the only colour in this monochrome place and they kick up a whirlwind of fine dust as they pass. Long ago, the streets would have been busy and noisy. Li tells us that 50 000 people once lived here, but today the donkey bells and rattling brays, the 'hip, hip' of their drivers and the whistling wind is all we hear. It is so dusty, the fine sand like beige flour as we trudge, following the cart tracks and there is little to see as far as decoration: just the endless bones of long dead buildings. It's a skeleton city.

'The local people stole the frescoes,' Li says, 'to fertilise their vine-yards.'

Let's hope that the lime and minerals provided a fine vintage or two. While China's dynasties have provided the weft, if you like, of the fabric of history, the warp has been the rich blend of cultures and nationalities in the country. The Han people are proud that they are by far the most numerous at around ninety-two per cent, making them the largest single human ethnic group in the world: about nineteen per cent of the world's population. This is quite a claim but, in many regions where other ethnic groups form the major part of the population, the 'minorities' seem anything but. In fact, China regards itself as multicultural with fifty-five ethnic minorities identified in the country.

We meet Naxi and Bai, Zhuang, Dai and Tibetan people as we travel. Each group varies enormously from the others in everything from clothing, customs, language and facial appearance to food and music. Just as in the West, these people's homes are also a key to ethnic differences.

Beyond the Yangtse River, but turning towards Tibet, we meet ladies with red scarves wrapped around their heads and over their mouths and others in more colourful costumes than the plain blue we have been seeing for days. Their houses are fascinating too, made from adobe, whitewashed between uprights, their walls leaning inwards at the top for greater strength we are told. The gabled roofs have no upward thrusting point on the ends as we had become used to seeing. On these the wooden shingles are weighed down with stones and each roof has a branch or a trident at the ends with a blue and white ragged flag fluttering.

Perhaps most striking is the method of drying hay in these parts. It appears to be just cut grass, but is hung on huge ladder-like frames and these dominate the outskirts of each village or stand in the fields like giant easels. They are surrounded by woven stick or straw fences to make sure, no doubt, that no one steals the precious hay, which is hoarded to feed the yaks through winter.

Further along a nomad family comes to check us out: grandma, the young mum and the kids. These people are so quiet and fearless, they just

筷
子

infiltrate whatever group is there and stand quietly absorbing it all. As we smile and nod, the mother settles down to feed the youngest on the bank in front of us without any embarrassment.

In cities, we often hear shy and self-conscious 'hellos' in English as we walk along. Many Chinese people want to speak English, but the opportunities are few. We speak to people in shops, take pictures of mundane things (causing some, I am sure, to say 'Wha-a-a-t!? Why would anyone want a picture of that?') or hang around as people play mahjong on the footpath. I watch one game and, when the only lady of the foursome is winning, I give her a thumbs-up sign making her smile broadly and almost lose track of her game.

The Zhuang people from Guangxi in the far south are the largest minority, (an estimated eighteen million) living in their own autonomous region and we glimpse some when visiting Guilin. The women's black headscarves and embroidered jackets, buttoned to the left, identify them, as do their baggy trousers and richly worked belts and shoes.

Further west we recognise the Uiygur people easily as their faces seem more European due to their proximity to Central Asia. Here the men wear stiff little embroidered caps and I have already mentioned how I found myself buying one—the cap, not the Uiygur man—in a market late one afternoon. The lady selling them told me she made them herself (now I have looked at it closely, I doubt that—sewing machines make different stitches to humans), but business was slow that day and I felt sorry for her. It was a wrong choice as it turned out to be too small for anyone in our family and, in any case, where would we wear a Uygyur cap, even if it did fit?

Beyond Urumchi, we visit Heavenly Lake. Here the Kazak people offer riding lessons for tourists on their glossy, feisty horses. The Russian name 'Cossack' comes from the Turkic word kazak, and means 'adventurer', another reminder of how near this corner of China is to Russia. These

筷子

people are known for their horsemanship and there is a corral nearby where we can hear whinnies and see occasional bursts of dust. From time to time a tourist with a Kazak guiding the horse carefully canters past.

While Gordon takes himself off to photograph all this, I wander by the lake. Suddenly, artlessly, a little girl around four years old in a frilly pink and white dress, red and gold cap and dainty embroidered pink vest just happens to pause in front of me. While Gordon is the official designated photographer in our group of two, I am never one to miss a photograph either, so I whip out my camera.

She is quicker though, waving a note in front of her pretty face before I can click. Oh, right! So this is a business deal is it? I pay her some yuan, she poses for me, strumming her mini-balalaika decorated with a tuft of owl feathers at the end and I take plenty of shots for my money. Nearby, her mother hovers ready to take the cash and adjust her child's ensemble for the next person who passes by.

Earlier that morning we peeped into a yurt in a Kazak village along the way to the lake and marvelled at the colourful interior. It was lined with multi-coloured woven and embroidered felt hangings, as richly impressive as stained glass in a cathedral.

Another time, on a boat in the middle of a lake near Dali, again in Yunnan, a troupe of Bai entertain us as we drink a selection of teas—described as bitter, sweet and aftertaste—from tiny porcelain cups. They explain that this traditional ceremony is a metaphor which stands for the three stages of life: bitter for early experiences, sweet (molasses and almond flakes) for the sweet parts of life and the spicy aftertaste (cinnamon and lemon) reflecting the later stages of life.

The women wear white trousers with a red embroidered waistcoat top over a white blouse and a red and white apron, lavish with gold and red embroidery. Each carries a wide red fan, as flimsy as a poppy's petal. On their heads they wear an embroidered white headdress, framing their face like a coronet, with a hank of white threads hanging to one side.

筷子

Like most cultural dance shows there is a complexity of dances, all with a legendary meaning, but I watch for another reason. I don't have two left feet—I say that I have three—and I watch any dancers, entranced as if it is a magic show, totally unable to begin to figure out how they do it.

As I sit there, lemon and spices stinging my lips, I reflect as I have been told to. Dynasties and minorities, it's all part of the dance that is China I figure. It's been a long performance, beginning four or five thousand years ago, but that's part of the magic of the place too.

筷子

# 18. USING CHOPSTICKS

*Better to be deprived of food for three days, than tea for one.*
**Chinese saying.**

'So, what was the food like?' This is one of the first questions almost everyone asks us when we return from Tibet.

Before we leave, some people long-facedly shake their heads and impress on me dreadful stories of illness and deprivation. I believe them so much that I pack a massive bottle of multi-vitamins just in case. In reality we find the cooler climate ideal for vegetable growing and probably eat more varieties there than we do at home.

All I discover about Tibetan food before I leave is that yak butter tea and tsampa, a mixture of toasted barley meal, which is equally an acquired taste, are staples. At one temple, we meet a monk sharing a mixture of yak cheese, butter, sugar and tsampa, moulded into a conical shape. One of our group tries it and, before the rest of us pluck up the courage, he recoils, saying it is revolting and rancid. We take his word on that.

In other places I see the churns used to make yak butter tea—tall bamboo containers with plungers that work the butter into the tsampa and tea—but I miss out on tasting it. Most of the locals I meet simply say it is nothing special, just ordinary butter mixed into ordinary tea. Maybe there is a reason for drinking it this way because, interestingly, I read somewhere that this concoction helps combat altitude sickness.

On my very last night in Lhasa I finally get to try tsampa and discover it is just a sweetish dough, rather like the edges of biscuit dough which we all scrounge as we cook.

Overall we eat extremely well on our trip. As we pass through China on the way into Tibet the restaurants are of course Chinese, but serve multitudes of dishes, many of them heavily hyped with chilli. The Tibetans seem to like their chilli and often offer it, chopped, as a condiment. We have yak meat on many occasions and it varies from tough and inedible to wonderful. Generally it is stir-fried or in a stew, but mostly meat is kept to a minimum. Tibetan Buddhists do not eat any 'small' animals, so fish and seafood—even if they were easily available—are taboo, but we do have chicken and pork from time to time.

Wine is not common in Tibet, but beer from local breweries is a very popular choice. We develop quite a taste for Lhasa beer. Of course you daren't drink the water, so bottled water is always available. Bread is usually round and flat, rather like a thick pita bread. One of my favourites is momo, a small steamed or fried pie or dumpling filled with meat or vegetables and similar to those found in many other cuisines.

Perhaps the best way to demonstrate the diet is to share the menu from the Snow Palace Restaurant in Lhasa, where we eat a final Tibetan meal the night before we fly home. We start with tsampa and the mandatory potato chips. It seems all Asia thinks anyone Western is addicted to them, because they bring them on even when they are not ordered.

Next comes a stew of something gristly, possibly sweet potato and yak, steamed rice, a grated carrot and meat stir-fry that is delicious and potato croquettes filled with meat, no doubt a form of momo. Two types of wilted, fried greens are brought—one something like a spinach, the other perhaps a water convolvulus—then a tomato and yak stew, shredded vegetables, a very hot dish of meat slices with chilli and finally a soup with huge chunks of turnip and meat. Dessert is usually ignored in Tibet, as it was at this meal.

For this occasion we sit on low-padded couches at square tables, helping ourselves from the huge number of dishes that just keep coming and coming. By this time we are getting quite adept at using chopsticks and manage (mostly) to transfer food from the platters to our plates without mishap. So while almost certainly no one plans a trip to Tibet just for the food, it is not to be feared or avoided either.

In other parts of China, we dine on mutton, pork or seafood, depending on where we are. This country is perhaps one of the birthplaces of regional food with dishes that have evolved over centuries making good use of local seasonal produce.

No one however, says that Chinese food is not confusing. Ever eaten ants climbing up a tree, braised lion's head or phoenix claw? You may have done so without realising it by tucking into dishes of minced pork stir-fried with glass noodles, pork meatballs or chicken's feet as they arrive at your table.

筷子

It is said that rice has been cultivated for over 8000 years in China and there are records of it being steamed in China from 800 BC, although it was used there for at least 2000 years before that. It was definitely grown in Egypt for 2500 years and today many countries still use it as their staple grain, although it was 1468 before Italy became the first country in Europe to enjoy it.

Apricots were mentioned in 2000 BC in China and there is talk of a sort of ice-cream made with snow from the mountains. This was emperor food—or more likely spoiled empress food—with servants being dispatched on fast horses to far flung places with orders to bring it back while it was still frozen. Or else! you would assume.

Peach, almond and olive trees were mentioned in China over 500 years before Christ and pumpkin is called 'the emperor of the garden'. Then there are Chinese gooseberries (kiwifruit), which are indigenous to forest margins in the Yangtse valley. The French name *souris vegetale* translates as 'plant mouse' because they feel the brown furry fruit resembles a mouse hanging by its tail.

While most modern vegetarians know the value of tofu, it has actually been on tables since 260 BC in China. Soya beans—one of the five ancient grains which has been grown for at least 2000 years in China—were known as 'meat of the earth'. The Japanese word tofu is adapted from the Chinese name, which literally means 'rotten beans'. All those of us who haven't developed a taste for it will heartily agree, although tofu—and indeed all other soy products—has been credited with the youthful looks enjoyed by older Asian women. This is an amazing selling point, when you think about the baby boomers. Someone sure missed the advertising boat with that angle.

The jury is still out on whether Marco Polo really did return to Italy with the know-how about noodles. Some say he didn't even go to China as some of his reports—flying horses, dragons, winged cats—are fanciful enough to make us think he may have been sidelined somewhere in la-la

筷
子

land. His cellmate may well have added extra details during Marco's imprisonment on his return to Italy. Rustichello was a 'romance writer' and penned Polo's autobiography, perhaps romancing a little too much about his new friend's travels. You can imagine him justifying his own journey into fantasy: 'after all who'll ever go there and find out it's not true?' Nonetheless specialty noodle shops certainly abounded in China by 960 AD and you imagine Polo would have lined up at least one lunchtime for a steaming bowlful.

Tea, for which China has become synonymous ('I wouldn't do that for all the tea in China!' was once an expression of absolute refusal) was supposedly discovered when some dried *camellia thea* leaves fell into the cauldron of water being prepared for sleepy Emperor Shen Nung of China in 2737 BC. He was delighted that drinking it helped him stay awake. It's a nice story, but you have to question the logistics. There would have had to be a large number of leaves falling into a cauldron and what was he doing sampling what was possibly meant to be his bath water?

Street food, of course is available everywhere throughout China, from satays grilling over charcoal burners to crusty golden breads filled with meat, which are cooked by sticking them barnacle-like on the inside of deep cylindrical stone ovens.

In various places we find corn, peanuts and chestnuts, which vendors fill into twists of newspaper, beside bowls of 1000-year-old eggs, their tanned and veined shells looking truly aged. At the gates of a temple in the south one rainy day, a man is frying potatoes whole, serving them stuck on a stick. We roll them in dried chilli and salt and devour them ravenously, declaring them comfort food at its finest.

In Urumchi we watch a man, wearing an Adidas cap, glazing star-shaped breads which he has just seconds before pulled from his oven at his outdoor bakery.

At Kashgar we loiter at a stall so we can watch as a family puts togeth-er a hearty meal for a customer. Their ingredients are all there and we

筷子

watch the cook in her white coat and apron cut slices of intestinal pieces from a bowl piled with sausage-like lengths filled with goodness knows what, along with stuffed stomach and liver, already boiled, then place them in a bowl with a lump of some yellow stuff which she hacks off a huge block. Closer inspection reveals it as a sort of doughy bread. To this selection she adds a hunk of lard. Next, good dashes of dried chillies, ground cumin, chopped onions, parsley and a decent slurp of soya sauce. She then ladles boiling broth over the whole mixture and presents it to her beaming patron.

Noodles seem to be available everywhere and one day, completely entranced, I watch a chef in a restaurant at Jiayuguang—at the far western end of the Great Wall—create a skein of fine noodles in seconds, adroitly folding and pulling, stretching and working what was such a short time ago just a shapeless lump of dough. It is as close to magic in a kitchen as you can get and I have yet to muster the time and courage to try it for myself.

The most notable feature of Chinese food is its variety. Apart from those for Islamic adherents, there are few religious taboos and this allows cooks to be very adventurous and innovative, ready to try anything and prepare it in any way possible. Regions and culture can affect life enormously and China's fifty-five ethnic minorities have very distinct ways with food.

For instance the Zhuang people—China's largest ethnic minority mainly located in the south-east—love to celebrate at festivals with strangely-named dishes such as torch pork, zijiang hare meat, fried pseudo-ginseng and spotted frogs.

To the west, in Xinjiang, the Islamic Uiygur people are forbidden to eat pork and some other meats, as well as blood. Mutton is a mainstay for them, as are the huge wheels of crusty bread called nang which are cooked in tandoor-like ovens.

In the north, the Manchu eat glutinous millet rice, buns, various pork and other meat dishes which are boiled or steamed.

筷
子

The Bai people, located to the south-west, specialise in making salted hams and sausages and even a snail sauce.

And of course, Szechuan is known for its tasty fiery dishes, but more on those later.

Towards Beijing the flavours mellow, although hotpots abound, no doubt having filtered down from the north, for some are still called Mongolian hotpots.

We encounter our first hotpot in Tianshui, where we are seated in a large restaurant with a small burner placed in front of us, along with small dishes of condiments: pieces of green capsicum, whole cloves of garlic, coriander and peanuts, as well as tiny saucers containing soya sauce with onion in it, chilli sauce and fish sauce. There is a slip of paper on our table: no doubt the order for our meal.

At the far end of the restaurant a young man makes crispy roti-style pancakes, a skilled business as they are as large as the barbecue plate on which he is cooking them. Deftly he spreads and flips them, then cuts them into pieces and delivers them to tables. They are so delicious we beg a second serving.

Someone appears with a pot of broth that is carefully placed over the burner, then come plates of cabbage, spinach, gourd and heaped plates of rolls of very thinly sliced beef and mutton and fresh white noodles. The staff hover to see if we know what to do, then mime that we must take some meat in our chopsticks then drop it into the soup for a few seconds. We are to lift it out, cool it and season it in the soya sauce. Then we are to do the same with the noodles and vegetables.

Cooking lesson over, we settle down to a new experience, having enormous fun playing with our food in this way, and discovering just how quickly the paper-thin meat slices cook. And while we exclaimed with shock at the amount of meat brought to us, we finish most of it with no trouble, mainly because we cannot resist adding just another few slices to the pot and watching them change colour as they cook in front of our eyes.

'This is the best meal ever,' Gordon exclaims at one point, his chin greasy from the broth that, after cooking so much meat and vegetables, has become a gloriously tasty soup.

As happens in life, the very next night after our train trip to X'ian, our guide excitedly meets us at the station with the news: 'I have a very special treat for you. Hotpot!'

The following night, in our bed and breakfast accommodation in the *hutong*, our hosts not only serve the dumplings I have helped create, but also treat us to hotpot, cooked this time in a home-style pot linked rather nattily by an extension cord to a power point in the ceiling.

Cantonese cooking in China's east is perhaps the French cuisine of this country with an amazingly extensive menu. Chinese food expert Kenneth Lo, in his *Regional Chinese Cookbook* describes the cuisine as 'one of the most refined, self-indulgent and degenerate in the whole of China!' It seems to have migrated most easily to other countries too and is often the one we encounter in Australian Chinese restaurants.

'Cantonese people eat everything except the table and chairs,' says our guide in Guilin and indeed Westerners are sometimes shocked at the different parts of animals put on the table in these areas, as well as the many unusual and exotic creatures that feature on menus.

But then, even if the ingredients are mainstream, there is nothing to stop the chefs getting fanciful when naming their dishes. I have a delightful book called *Chinese Culinary*—bought in Sydney's Chinatown twenty-five years ago—optimistically subtitled 'in plain English' although it turns out to be anything but. The author, W Sou San, has included useful recipes for such dishes as Prodigal Chicken, Phoenix Merry-Making, Buddha's Cushion, Purity of Devotion and one that is sure to catch on: Chastity Cake. There are others that you would have to have grown up loving, such as braised eel bladder and braised groper skin.

While we all recognise *chow mein* on the menu, you may not know that *chop suey* was actually created by Chinese immigrants to America last

筷
子

century and literally means 'bits and pieces', no doubt an ideal way to use up leftovers.

I am sure W Sou San would back this frugality. In his final chapter he exhorts cooks to make use of scraps, saying 'many a housewife develops bad moods because she has nothing to cook, but if organised to a stream-line you would be surprised how many things could be utilised for a wholesome meal', advising her to lay in stocks of noodles and a 'few cans of corned beef for emergency rations'.

Fortunately cooks in China don't rely on canned food because early each morning, at every market in the land, they will be there selecting dew-fresh vegetables and haggling over meat which is often hacked off the carcass to order. At one market in Kashgar we saw chickens selected, their necks wrung then plunged immediately into vats of boiling water to loosen the feathers and make them easier for the plucking. All this happened within minutes of their cackling, loudly-protested deaths.

The Chinese, like many Asian people, are particularly fastidious about the fish and seafood they eat and this holds true wherever they migrate as well. If you are lucky enough to live in a neighbourhood with many Chinese or other Asian residents you can almost bet that the local seafood seller has been instructed that only the best and freshest fish will do.

Texture is important in Chinese dishes too and vegetables such as water chestnuts and celery or nuts, such as almonds, see to that. Flavour is paramount and most dishes are served in a subtle sauce, often thickened with cornflour. Generally diners in the Szechuan and Honan areas prefer much hotter food than other regions of China and I can attest to this because of a 'near-death' experience in Chengdu.

It is nearly the end of our trip and the entire group of us—possibly ten or twelve—are assembled around the white-clothed table with the traditional huge turntable in the centre: a clone of those found in every major restaurant throughout the land and in Chinese restaurants the world over, on which are placed the long procession of dishes.

筷子

I knew we could expect hot food in this region, but am totally unprepared for one dish. As I bite into a piece of chicken a burst of the chilli-hot oil, in which it has been cooked, hits a sensitive part of my throat and suddenly it's as if my ears have ignited too, but from the inside. For at least a minute the intense oily heat seems to consume my entire head and, unable to make a sound, I think 'here am I dying' while the others around me continue their unconcerned lunchtime chatter.

We have a similar experience at Tianshui, along the Silk Road. At a clay-pot restaurant the waiter brings us an absolutely delicious dish of prawns and calamari with quails' eggs. The sauce is silky and studded with small, pinkish, dried berry-like things that have been deep fried and are delightfully crunchy. They are so good in fact, that I pick them out specially to nibble on and before long discover my tongue and lips are numbing, as if I have just been to the dentist.

In countries like China you have no control over what goes into any dish you eat. You can plead for there to be no MSG, you can enquire about the provenance or the content of your meal and at best you will receive a beautiful smile and a nod. Food sensitivities are not greatly catered for once you get off the beaten track. If you want to give yourself something to worry about, all you have to do is imagine that maybe some unfamiliar texture or shape represents the one food you have never as yet eaten, the one that will bring on a massive reaction.

It is folly to do that however, because that would mean missing some exhilarating experiences and a lot of great eating. Generally, it's best to simply wade in with your chopsticks and try everything in sight. Some things, like those Szechuan peppercorns, I treat with caution. *Zanthoxylum piperitum* is not a true peppercorn, but rather the shells from the berry of the prickly ash tree and a component of five-spice powder.

On the health-food scene, China pioneered the use of soya beans and the making of tofu and bean curd—which can be seen drying in the sun in some parts of the country—long before Australia was discovered.

筷子

Gluten, the protein part of wheat, which is extracted by washing flour until only the rubbery gluten mass remains, created a meat-like substitute centuries ago. Today a vegetarian can dine on a huge array of dishes in most areas of China. One Chinese belief says that abstaining from meat during the last significant moments of the Old Year purifies body and soul. It may be worth adopting, if only for the final five minutes of each year.

Stir-frying, along with steaming and deep-frying, is perhaps the cooking method used most to prepare food in restaurants and at home. The shape of woks varies between the north, where pans have two handles, and the south of China where they feature one longer handle. Chinese say they like to sit near the kitchen because it is from this vantage point that they 'get the breath of the wok'. Certainly this quick method prevents the loss of vitamins that are destroyed by prolonged high heat. Steaming, commonly done in bamboo steamers, often stacked several layers high, also preserves nutrients.

Chinese food is essentially very healthy. Ingredients are fresh, prepared quickly using simple cooking methods that don't lose too many vitamins and minerals and the food is eaten immediately. Dishes are often low-fat, high in fibre, low in refined ingredients and rely extensively on fresh foods and complex carbohydrates. There is also an emphasis on white meat and seafood, especially fish and sea vegetables in some regions.

Chinese meals do not usually make a feature of desserts, diners often simply preferring a piece of fresh seasonal fruit. Even bread, cakes and biscuits are not generally consumed in the same quantities that Westerners are accustomed to and coffee drinking is limited, although an endless stream of green tea is consumed with every meal. Research suggests this is a good thing due to the antioxidants it contains.

While sugar is not used much, I remember an amazing dish at a Tibetan-run place in Lan Zhou. While the decor was atmospheric and the walls beautifully hung with Tibetan rugs and decorated with artefacts and brilliantly coloured pictures and although the staff, in traditional dress,

筷子

grouped together and sang to us at the conclusion of the meal, I remember most just one dish. It was very simple, but totally and unexpectedly good. Chunks of fried potatoes had been drizzled with toffee, just before serving. Yes, toffee! I dreamed about that dish and when we returned there a couple of days later, I begged for it again. And it was just as good.

Who was the first person in Asia to use sticks to pick up their food? No one knows, but the Chinese words can mean 'nimble fingers' even though many Westerners feel anything but when using them.

The original term was pronounced fie *shee* but 'shee' sounds like death and it became especially taboo to utter the words on ships as no one wanted to talk about a quick death there, so the name was altered slightly. Even today it is bad manners to stand your chopsticks in the rice in your bowl as this is what is done at funerals.

Travelling through China is like attending a sumptuous banquet, so rich, varied and plentiful that there is no way anyone can sample it all, whether you use chopsticks or not.

# 19. ON THE TOURIST TRAIL

*Each generation will reap what the former generation has sown.*

**Chinese Proverb**

Two small boys at the lake's edge put down their chopsticks and stop eating. They rummage in a bag beside them and hold up what look like small eggs in their hands. The stones are wet and when they roll them in front of me, I see a flashing blue light deep within.

'They are moonstones,' an older person nearby says. 'The boys have brought them up from the bottom of the lake.'

It is such a magical thought that these perfectly shaped stones have been recovered just that morning from Lake Er Hai's deep waters. I buy three at a dollar each, immediately.

Later, I wonder if this story is strictly true. Moonstone is a soft milky white stone, a sort of feldspar, but valuable because of its beauty. It picks up surrounding colours and somehow beams them out from its heart. I doubt that it occurs spontaneously already egg-shaped, as if laid by a deep-water mythical beast and I suspect the boys have dipped the tumbled rocks in water to showcase them and enhance their beautiful tones. Maybe they are targeting tourists because—in addition to the fact they have ready cash for change—moonstone has been called 'the traveller's stone' because it is thought to offer them protection.

I really don't care about any of this. At home I display my stone in water in a small glass and its blue greeting when I pick it up it never fails to remind me of a happy day we spent on a blue lake, near Dali, in China's south-west.

Er Hai Lake is a high altitude lake, part of the catchment area for the mighty Mekong that flows south through several south-east Asian countries before finally exiting via its massive delta in Vietnam. It is one of the seven biggest fresh water lakes in China and the name simply means, 'a sea shaped like an ear' because of its size and shape of around 400 square kilometres.

We arrive at the dock early and find several large passenger boats already moored there. Our catamaran can take 500 passengers we are told and, while we wait to board, I check the stalls along the waterfront, of course! I notice an interesting change in the goods on offer here: multitudinous strings of red glass chillies made to hang as decorations or wear as pendants. I buy a few for gifts then find myself in an argument with one shopkeeper. Rather the Chinese around him are haranguing him and, I think, accusing him of over-charging. It turns out that it is simply a language problem. I am guilty of attempting to buy around forty of them—well, they looked like they were in a set—for the price of one.

That sorted, I take my embarrassment and my chillies and board the boat, heading for the top deck, where a delightful crew of Bai maidens and young men dressed in traditional red and white embroidered outfits, play horns and cymbals to greet us. The lake this morning is serene and still, so motionless that the far mountains are reflected in it, but we discover later on the trip that, because the lake is so large, there are times when we can see no land at all.

We know we are in Tourist Land because of the type of tour, but the other tourists are mainly Chinese, so we feel better about that. In fact that is the way it is in most places we visit in China. The huge local population, as well as Chinese from other countries who come back to see their land of origin, means that the more popular sites are almost always packed with visitors. There are an estimated 34 million Overseas Chinese, mainly resident in south-east Asian countries, who are counted in China's 1.3 billion headcount.

We stop at one island in the lake, called Golden Chateau, and walk up to the pagoda. This whole area is the land of the Bai people whose warlords once ruled this remote area and the building is a typical ancient Chinese Buddhist temple with pointed, tipped-up corners on the tiled roof and minutely carved wooden eaves meticulously crafted and painted. Whoever did this must have used every colour in his paint box, and would surely have stood back and nodded in approval when he finished.

Of course there are more people here too, trying to sell us anything: bracelets, more chilli pendants (cheaper too), dried fish and prawns, bowls of noodles, embroidered purses, vests, carved marble and there are baskets filled with dried eels, curled in grotesque shapes, which I am happy to leave right there. On the way back to the boat, I meet my little friends with their magic booty.

About as far south, but many hundreds of kilometres away in Guangxi province near Guilin, we board another boat. Most people recognise pictures of the unusual limestone karst formations and peaks of this region which were thrust up 300 million years ago. It looks as if a giant has dropped a green and blue sheet over a crowd of people, who stand like a cast waiting for their cue to move on-stage. From the air as we fly in though, we could be diving over coral or suspended over stalagmites in a cavern.

'This whole area was only opened to tourism in 1975,' says the guide, telling us that in the six months before we arrive there have been 4.8 million visitors to the area.

筷
子

She reels off figures in the billions of yuan. No wonder tourism is now the number one industry here. The Li River is sold to these visitors as 'a hundred miles of river, a hundred miles of picture galleries' because many rock formations on the banks can be interpreted as something else, usually with a legendary or poetic connotation by the tour commentators.

We've just enjoyed a busy few days in Shanghai and I am looking forward to a leisurely, quiet ride on the river. As we park and move towards the wharf, I realise that my 'peaceful river trip' will not be quite so tranquil. The car park is crammed with big fifty-two seater buses and there is a convoy of boats waiting at the dock, filling fast.

Once on the water, I count fourteen boats like ours in sight, possibly more beyond the bend of the river and the noise of fourteen amplified commentaries mingled with the thrum of the motors doesn't allow much reverie. In addition, there seems to be some sort of hooter language between the boats. Once one lets go a huge 'whoomp' the others respond, until I feel the rocks will soon reverberate like organ pipes.

The mountains thrust up in stony silence beside the river. In parts when it narrows to around fifty metres, we are close enough to see the low bushes and creepers gripping tenaciously to the almost vertical sides. It's a misty day and the progression towards the furthest formations resembles the range of greys on a paint chart.

The water is jade green and we pass people in small boats snacking on bowls of something or other, as they seem to do anywhere, anytime in China. Others wash clothes on the river's edge. There are ducks, ducklings and the occasional bamboo raft. Huck Finn eat your heart out, I think.

The commentary encourages us to see a woman carrying her baby and yearning for her husband's return in one far rock formation or a massive painting of nine horses on a cliff face. We squint obediently, but all I seem to find are snails and stooped old men, fingers, maybe an elephant and perhaps a dragon. I could be persuaded that one range resembled knuckles or even a row of teeth, but a pen rack, as we are enthusiastically prompted to see in another set of mountains? Not sure about that.

Our boat is very clean and air-conditioned. The seats, covered with plaid fabric, look as though they have come direct from a VW that has gone to the great caryard in the sky. They look rather smart, as do the gold velvet curtains.

We stop at a market town of course, so we can buy stone 'chops' (stamps) carved with the Chinese equivalent of our names and one for each of our children and more for anyone else we can think of. It all takes a long time and each is carefully wrapped in a scrap of newsprint, and locked into a small cardboard box with the ribbon and plastic rod latch, so beloved of Asian packagers.

While we wait I have a conversation with a small child and use a word I have just picked up.

'Your name, Mai Li,' I say, meaning she is beautiful.

She eyes me solemnly, then clearly and with great dignity replies: 'Sank you.'

That evening, after dinner, we return to the waterfront in Guilin. The night market is still in full swing, but we are going fishing—cormorant fishing—another tourist display.

'One cormorant is as good as three good fishermen,' the fisherman in a scuffed blue cap and baggy jacket tells us. He is seated on a bamboo raft, surrounded by his five cormorants which he tells us cost him 10 000 yuan each. There are quite a few of us here and we have each paid 80 yuan for a forty-five minute show, so I do some quick maths and figure he can buy a new bird for every 125 people who watch them ... and that's without selling the fish!

These birds are like pets, he says. He has raised them since they hatched and they will always return to him. Which is the point of course, because first he must go out a little distance, shine a light downwards to attract the fish and utter a fair imitation of a cormorant cry to launch them into the water.

From here on the cormorants do what they were made to do and go after the fish, but they cannot swallow them as they should when they catch them because the wily owner has tied a piece of straw around their throats. Instead, they return to the boat and the man pulls out the fish, adding to his haul.

'If they catch small ones, they can swallow,' he says, and we see a few receive a minute treat or two.

I feel sorry for the cormorants, although they seem happy enough. I know I wouldn't thank anyone to pull food out of my mouth. Particularly if I'd had to dive into cold water in the dark to get it.

No discussion of tourism in China would be complete without a mention of the Great Wall. There are many myths about it (no, it cannot be seen from outer space) but none come close to the reality of this 6700-kilometre long structure which is well over 2000 years old. Its construction employed hundreds of thousands of workers—300 000 in one era and another 1.8 million in another—and took hundreds of years to complete. Today it draws millions of visitors each year.

The Great Wall was declared a UNESCO World Heritage site in 1987 and nothing in the world comes close to it for its sheer daring ambition

and endurance. Of course we have to see it and set off on an uncharacter-
istically—that's what locals tell us anyway—sunny, golden, balmy
autumn Beijing morning. Soon I find myself sitting on the Great Wall of
China, built primarily as a defence to keep the barbarians of the north
from coming down and snatching away the silk and other precious goodies from the south.

There are a few trampling hordes today, not from the north, but
hiking up and down the top of the wall itself, which is as wide as a street.
Somewhere I read that it has an average height of ten metres and a width
of five metres. When there is a break in the pedestrian traffic I hear gentle
massage-room music coming from a loudspeaker mounted somewhere
nearby in bushes which are already showing a flash of autumn colour.

Everyone's here: pushy Germans (twice I have been elbowed aside by
them), Aussies (I know because of a koala hanging from their backpack)
and multitudes of Chinese of course, proud of this ancient dragon that has
protected their country for centuries. It was once regarded as impregnable.

'Anyone who could climb the Wall,' says our guide Jane, 'was a hero.'

She doesn't mean climbing the way we have come though, by cute
blue and orange plastic 'sliding cars' from the car park far below for
US$10 return.

By the look of the Wall most tourists have felt impelled to inscribe
their names on it, but I can't read most of the graffiti because it is in
Chinese characters. Nearer to the entrance there are the inevitable sellers
of T-shirts and caps with 'I Climbed the Great Wall' on them, silk paintings, gold coins and badges, jade carvings and bottled drinks, but higher
up there is none of this junk and the air is pure and clean.

Like so many others here today we stroll along in the sunshine, caught
up in the thrill of finally being here. Gordon takes a multitude of pictures,
we snap each other hanging out and waving through holes in the wall, then
stop and gaze over boundless hills and ranges. We try to trace with our eyes
the sinuous loops and curves of this stony fortress-wall wandering almost

筷子

aimlessly it appears, off towards the hazy horizon and wonder at the vision that even began to imagine it.

A couple of weeks later we arrive at the far end of the Great Wall, at Jiayuguang, the far end of the kingdom. This fortification, known as 'the impregnable pass under heaven' and built to guard the Hexi corridor, was begun in 1372 AD and took 168 years to build. It is said the plans were so exact that only one brick was left over and it remains on display. Now the fort has been restored to remarkable condition.

The guide translates the words placed here in the fifteenth century outside the Trap Court Gate: 'people should collect here to show passports'. There is nothing new in travel it seems.

We spend a while here, wandering the quiet courtyards under the imposing pagoda-shaped towers, imagining it as it once must have been. We look up as a jet trail inscribes a white exclamation mark above the ancient brick walls. Yet another metaphor for China.

In March 1974, a simple farmer was digging a well in his pomegranate orchard near X'ian, the official beginning of the Silk Road. Mr Yang must have wondered what his spade had hit because no one had ever seen anything quite like the object he unearthed. This was no wonder as the terracotta warriors were fired in the Qin dynasty and had been buried for 2000 years.

We join a queue to see them the day after we arrive in the city, shuffling forward with hundreds of others. Like the Wall it is something you must see when you visit China or you will forever be disappointed.

Seven hundred craftsmen were employed to make these figures which are still being dug up and pieced together. It is said they worked in twos, fashioning the features by looking at each other's faces. The warriors were created larger than life to show their status, although the chariots were half size, and they were fired in 20 charcoal-heated kilns.

The entire display area is also an archaeological site and every evening, when the crowds are locked out, a team of thirty archaeologists clock on and begin the painstaking nightly task—from 6pm until midnight—of matching fragments of terracotta to create an entire body.

I guess this is my greatest surprise. Having seen displays of the warriors, I somehow believed that they had been sealed up undamaged in a tomb. But time and human interference along the centuries has reduced some to thousand-piece jigsaws.

The pits hold torsos separated from heads, arms tossed aside or legs awkwardly out of place. It looks like a battlefield, which is fitting as these figures were crafted initially as warriors. As we use the walkways over and around the pits, I feel great amazement and gratitude that these people, the archaeologists, are so careful and patient.

In another pit a small battalion stands complete except for their heads. Further along we find the long ranks of warriors, complete with horses, that we recognise from pictures in magazines. The whole site is housed in a huge hangar-like auditorium, home to the 6000 or so warriors and we walk around it, marvelling at the extent of it all. The lights are kept low to preserve the army. Where the archaeologists are working, there is a haze of dust in the air and, while most people murmur as if in church, it seems strange to hear mobile phones ringing out over 2000-year-old statues.

This is a massive moneymaking project for China, netting about a billion yuan (around A$150million) a year from the estimated ten million visitors. A proportion of this comes from the books and souvenirs, which include replica warriors made from the discarded clay from the diggings. It's a nice touch though, a good selling point (well, it got us in) and as good an example of recycling as you'll find.

In the gift shop at the end of our tour, I buy a book outlining the history of the monumental—in more ways than one—task of bringing these warriors to light. Because it is Saturday—and because this is an amazing country given to unexpected discoveries, coincidences and chance encounters—I am told that I may have it signed by an unassuming

筷子

elderly gentleman with a wispy beard, seated at a table nearby. To my delight it turns out to be the man responsible for it all: Mr Yang himself.

This book is finished, now: such a small taste of this rich, varied and plentiful land. There is really only one thing left for you to do now: go and see for yourself!

Perhaps it is best to close with yet another Chinese proverb, this time from the great man himself and leave it at that.

*Wheresoever you go: go with all your heart.*
**Confucius**

筷子

筷子

# VISITING CHINA

Visiting China today is far simpler than it has ever been, but there are still some things to know.

Foreign tourists require visas, which usually allow a 30-day stay in the country.

Mandarin is the official language of China. Several other languages and dialects are spoken throughout the country, however English is taught in schools and many people like to practise their English when they meet a foreigner.

Self-driving is still very difficult in China because of the traffic and sign-posting. Hiring a driver and car or booking an organised guided tour either by road or boat will allow you to see more and be more relaxed. The Chinese rail system is convenient and the 'soft' class offers greater comfort. China also has a number of domestic airlines that fly to regional centres.

No special vaccinations are required for visitors from uninfected areas. Standard medications are available, although you should bring your own prescription medicines. There is some malaria risk in the southern and southeastern provinces. Drink bottled water at all times.

Keep receipts for gold, silver and precious gems bought in China to show Customs if required on leaving the country. Make sure you have authorisation and a red wax seal on any antiques you plan to take home.

筷子

Most major currencies are accepted for exchange and most major credit cards are accepted in shops and larger restaurants. There are approximately 6 renminbi (RMB) to the Australian dollar. Tipping is becoming more accepted.

The best time to visit most provinces isgenerally between April and October. Winter months in the north and at higher altitudes may be very cold, so pack accordingly.

Electricity is 220 volts and the plug types may vary. Carry a set of adaptor plugs if you plan to use your own electrical appliances.

All China operates on Beijing time, which is two hours behind Australian EST (Eastern Standard Time).

Restrictions may apply for taking photographs in temples and museums. Taking pictures from the air of bridges, military personnel and installations is also forbidden. If in doubt, ask.

China is a shopper's paradise and many goods may be bargained for, especially in markets. Larger stores, including government-run and 'friendship' stores usually have fixed prices. When buying larger items, enquire about shipping costs to your home.

Chinese food varies according to the region. Expect Muslim influences in the west; hotter food in Szechuan; hot pots, Peking duck and dumplings in Beijing and seafood, pork, chicken and rice dishes in Canton, towards the south.

筷
子

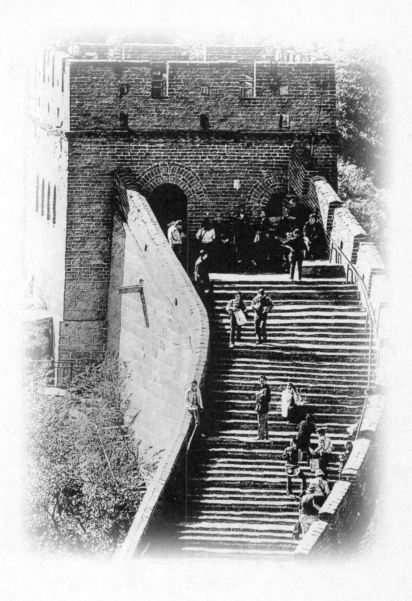

筷子

# CHOPSTICK ETIQUETTE

**HOLDING THEM:**

There are various ways but this works for me:

Position your chopsticks so that the lower one fits in the angle between your thumb and first finger. Rest it on the tip of your ring finger and hold it steady with the lower part of your thumb.

Do not hold them in the middle or the front third. Hold them well back. Position the other chopstick above it and rest it between the tips of your first and middle fingers. Hold it in place with the tip of your thumb. That way you can manipulate both to pick up even tiny pieces of food – right down to a grain of rice, although it takes some practice. As that usually involves eating Chinese food, you will have a lot of fun along the way.

**THE POLITE WAY TO EAT:**

Never pass food to someone else's chopsticks with your chopsticks or leave your chopsticks sticking up from food, especially rice. Both these actions are associated with death and funerals.

When not eating, place your chopsticks in front of you with the tip facing left.

Use chopsticks like tongs to pick up pieces of food. Do not spear food with them.

It is considered bad manners to wave chopsticks around or point them at others.

If a serving plate has no serving spoon, use the thick end of your own chopsticks (rather than using the end you have been eating with) to serve yourself with food.

It is good manners to lift a rice bowl to your mouth and shovel the rice in with your chopsticks.

筷
子

Keep your hand facing downwards when using chopsticks. Showing your palm is considered unrefined.

**DID YOU KNOW?**

A common wedding present in China is a set of chopsticks. Not only is this practical, but the Chinese word for chopsticks sounds the same as 'soon son'.

筷子

筷子

*Woman selling cabbages*

筷子

190

# CHINESE FOOD

## WHAT IS IT?

While Chinese cuisine calls for many of the same ingredients used in Western cookery, some may be unfamiliar. Whole books have been written on this subject, but here are just a few you may come across in this book or other recipes.

## HERBS AND SPICES

**Coriander**: Chinese parsley or cilantro. Used in many Asian and Indian dishes. Leaves and roots are used for different flavours. Seeds, whole or ground, are called for in other dishes.

**Cumin:** may be used ground or in seeds.

**Curry leaves:** available dried from Asian stores.

**Five spice powder:** a blend of star anise, fennel, cloves, cinnamon and Szechuan pepper. Use sparingly. Does not keep well.

**Lemongrass:** long thin grass-like stalks, available sometimes in vegetable markets, but more often in Asian shops. Powder is available, but is not as fresh and pungent. Dried stalks sometimes available.

**Lime leaves:** available fresh or dried from Asian stores.

**Szechuan pepper or sansho:** ground prickly ash, numbs lips and tongue if not used sparingly.

**Turmeric:** adds colour and flavour. Mainly used ground, although fresh in Asian markets.

**Vietnamese mint:** has a hot coriander flavour. Available for home planting and fresh in Asian markets, but not commercially available dried or powdered.

## SAUCES

**Black bean sauce**: very salty, available commercially.

**Fish sauce:** available bottled from Asian stores.

**Hoisin:** used as Westerners would use tomato sauce or barbecue sauce. Available bottled.

筷子

**Plum sauce:** a sweet chutney-like sauce which adds flavour to dishes.

**Soya sauce:** the light soya sauce has more flavour, but is thinner and weaker looking. Dark soya sauce is sweeter and thicker. Both are very salty although there are salt-reduced brands.

## OILS

**Dark sesame oil:** strongly flavoured oil made from roasted sesame seeds. Use sparingly.

**Vegetable oil:** any good quality nut or seed oil may be used. Peanut oil is used in many recipes.

## LEGUMES

**Black beans:** black soya beans with similar nutrition to the more common soya beans. Available canned or as a sauce, but very salty.

**Peanuts:** used in many dishes—either whole and cooked as for other legumes—roasted and ground as an addition to satays or roasted whole as a garnish.

**Soya beans:** this versatile bean is available in a variety of forms including tofu and dried beancurd, the latter often available in long yellow sticks or sheets.

## GRAINS AND FLOURS

**Cornflour:** often used to thicken sauces and dishes. Stir a little into a small amount of cold water until dissolved. Slowly pour into boiling liquid and stir until clear and thickened.

**Gluten:** the protein part of wheat used to make a meat substitute.

**Noodles:** a wide variety are used in many dishes. Many are available packaged in supermarkets, ready to cook and eat within a few minutes.

**Bean or glass vermicelli:** made from mung beans and are fine and clear and often dried.

**Hokkien, Singapore, mee:** often sold ready to use in Asian stores.

筷
子

**Rice noodles or bee hoon**: straight white sticks in packets, in Asian stores or health food shops or sold fresh in packets.

**Rice:** an extensive mainstay of most Asian meals. There are many varieties and uses, from white polished rice to red, black and glutinous or 'sticky' rice.

**Wrappers:** spring roll wrappers are tough, thin and used to wrap a wide variety of fillings before deep frying. Available fresh from Asian stores. Store frozen or refrigerated.

**Wonton wrappers:** small squares of thin and pliable pasta dough, usually incorporating eggs, are sold in packets in Asian stores. May be stored frozen or refrigerated.

## VEGETABLES

Asian cookery uses vegetables extensively. Carrots, onions, asparagus, peas, beans, corn, celery, cauliflower, zucchini, capsicum, broccoli, cucumber, garlic are all common to Western as well as Eastern cuisine. Below is a list of more unusual vegetables used often in oriental cookery.

**Bamboo shoots:** available canned, whole or sliced. Drain and use as needed. Store in water or liquid in a screw-top jar in the fridge for up to a month or freeze for up to 12 months.

**Bean sprouts:** mostly available fresh in vegetable markets in packets, also available canned.

**Bok choy, on choy, wam buk:** all members of the Chinese cabbage family. Sold in bunches, often used interchangeably.

**Chestnuts:** these are available dried and need to be stored airtight and rehydrated before use.

**Chillies:** small red, fiery ones are used extensively. Use gloves to protect hands and skin and do not touch eyes or lips after handling without washing hands first. Discard seeds to minimise fieriness. Crushed chillies are available, bottled. This prevents the need to handle the fiery little

筷子

things. Also available as a paste, in sauces or powdered. If hot green chillies are called for and not readily available fresh, use Jalapeno chillies, sold canned in Mexican food shops.

**Corn:** mini corn is available canned or fresh and adds interest to stirfry dishes.

**Ginger:** available fresh in most vegetable markets. Peel and grate or slice thinly. May be frozen in which case it is easier to skin by placing under very hot water and peeling skin off. Store at room temperature for short periods: up to two weeks before use.

**Green onions:** sometimes incorrectly called spriing onions or shallots. Long, thin green onions, used in many dishes.

**Lotus roots:** available dried in Asian stores. Rehydrate before use. Store airtight.

**Mushrooms:** Chinese or shiitake. Available fresh but more commonly dried. They are black, shrivelled and expensive, but only a few are needed for flavour. Soak in hot water for about 30 minutes, remove stem as it is inedible, before slicing caps thinly unless recipe calls for another method. Soaking water may be used as part of the sauce for added flavour.

**Cloud ear or wood fungus:** need soaking to allow them to swell. Not a strong flavour but they absorb the flavours of other foods.

**Oyster:** sometimes available fresh. A delicate flavour for use in salads or stirfries.

**Snow peas:** pods of tiny immature peas that are 'top and tailed' and then cooked whole or sliced and usually stir-fried.

**Water chestnuts:** available canned, whole or sliced. Drain and use as needed. Store as for bamboo shoots.

## FRUIT

Pineapple and watermelon are commonly in Chinese dishes. Here are some others:

筷子

**Coconut:** used widely in many recipes and available desiccated, shredded, flaked, or canned—as coconut cream or milk— or dried as milk powder

**Lychees:** small sweet, white fruits in a firm red skin, available fresh or canned. Use in sweet or savoury dishes.

## OTHER

**Agar agar:** a dried white powder made from seaweed and used to thicken and gel liquids. Must be added to a little warm water, boiled for one minute, then added to warm ingredients. Sets at room temperature.

**Mirin:** rice wine or vinegar.

筷子

# WOK TALK

Once a wok was an exotic piece of equipment in Australia. Today it is a standard accessory. The unique shape of a wok—which concentrates heat at the base where it is most effective—makes for speedy cooking, and allows food to retain much of its natural colour, flavour and nutrients.

Woks have been used in China for at least 3000 years. Originally designed for use over primitive wood or charcoal fires, the wok is equally at home here and now. The reason is simple: tasty food retaining its natural texture and flavour is always in style.

When buying a wok, look first in an Asian supply store where the woks will often be better quality and less expensive than in a kitchen shop or department store. If possible buy woks of different sizes for large and small dishes. If you use gas, also buy a stabilising ring for the pan. Woks will work on electric hotplates, but seem to perform best with gas. A wok with a frypan-handle on one side is good, and even better if there is a small one on the opposite side. A wok full of hot food can sometimes be heavy and tricky to manipulate one-handed.

Before using your wok for the first time, wash it well with hot soapy water. This should be the last time that you will ever wash it. Dry it, then wipe oil all over the inside and outside. Place it over a high heat for ten or more minutes to allow the oil to burn off. Wipe off all the excess burned oil with a paper kitchen towel then store the pan in a dry place. After each use, wipe out the wok or rinse it very lightly then dry. Initially, rub a light film of oil over the wok before putting it away, but after prolonged use there should be a build-up of 'seasoning' on the pan and you will not need to continue oiling it.

筷子

Before cooking, place some oil in the base of the pan and let it get quite hot. Always cook over a high heat. When stir-frying—because cooking time is so quick—make sure that all ingredients are prepared beforehand and do not leave the wok. You should be free to lift and turn the food the whole time so that it cooks evenly.

When adding liquids, pour them down the side of the pan so that they heat as they run in and don't form a pool of cooler liquid in the base. It is essential that the food stays at an even heat. If it loses heat, it can begin to steam and vegetables will lose their characteristic crunchy-crisp texture.

Always add the longest-cooking foods first: onions, carrot, capsicum, celery and finish with foods that need the least—snow peas, green onions, bean sprouts, herbs and mushrooms. Add new ingredients by clearing a space in the base where they may heat quickly while the food on the sides stays warm without further cooking.

Woks are not only useful for stir-frying. Put two chopsticks across the pan and balance a steamer or plate on them to cook food more gently. The wok may be used for poaching, stewing or simmering food or even to smoke food.

筷子

# HOW TO COOK RICE

Rice almost triples in quantity when cooked. A cup of dry rice can swell to almost three cups when cooked and serve four or more people. Try cooking rice using stock or coconut milk for variety.

Cook white rice in plenty of boiling water (salted if you like) for 15 minutes, or until tender, then drain. There should be no need to rinse it. Commercial electric rice-cookers are extremely popular with people who eat rice daily, but a simple plastic one which cooks rice in the microwave, also works well.

Prepare sticky rice by soaking overnight in water to cover, then draining and steaming for 30–45 minutes. The resulting sticky mass is suitable for chilling, cutting into shapes or for use in recipes that call for it specifically.

### FRIED RICE

This is one of the most basic of all Asian meals and a wonderful way to use up leftovers attractively. For firm, separate grains, cook rice the day before and refrigerate it—covered—in a shallow dish overnight or for several hours.

To cook, simply heat a little oil in a large pan, add chopped onions, garlic, fresh ginger, chopped chilli, capsicum, mushrooms and any other vegetables you like. Stir in a beaten egg if liked, mixing it through well, then add cooked or raw chopped meat, chicken or fish and basically anything you like.

Stir until everything is heated through and meat is cooked and browning. Season to taste with salt or soya sauce and chilli. Again, do it according to your own taste and imagination. Finally add rice and stir to combine it with the other ingredients. Let it heat right though and a become little crispy on the bottom if you like.

## RICE STORAGE

Rice is easy to store and may be kept for several months airtight in a cool dry place. In warmer months it may be refrigerated or stored in the freezer to discourage insect pests. Some varieties from Asian countries may need to be washed before use or checked for stones. Australian rice needs no rinsing.

Once rice has been cooked it should be kept refrigerated and covered. It will keep this way for several days or may be frozen successfully for up to a month. The texture may change and become more crumbly, so decide whether this will matter in the finished dish or if it is just as easy to cook fresh rice.

筷子

# RECIPES

The cuisine of China is so varied and extensive. This is just a small sampling of dishes we ate as we travelled the country.

As you try them use your wok and chopsticks and think of this enormpous land that has shared so much with the world.

# HOT POT

This classic dish can vary enormously depending on what you have on hand. All meat needs to be shaved paper thin. You can do this by partially freezing meat or chicken then slicing it extremely finely with a very sharp knife. It can be marinated as desired or used the way it is. Alternatively buy meat ready-sliced and frozen from Asian supermarkets.

A special pot is not necessary as any deep saucepan can be used, but you will need a small burner or hotplate so you can cook and eat at the table. Plan to have no more than four people for each average sized pot and burner.

Use stock for the pot and arrange spicy condiments so each diner can mix his or her own dipping sauce to taste. The stock in the pot will become tastier as the meats are cooked in it and can be enjoyed as a soup at the end of the meal.

### TO SERVE:

Heat 1–1½ litres of stock in a deep saucepan, to about two-thirds full, on a table burner or hotplate in the middle of the table so everyone can reach it easily. Add more as the meal continues to keep the level the same.

Arrange plates containing sliced meats, dumplings, fish balls, halved mushrooms and other vegetables cut into strips, fresh noodles, tofu, eggs and anything else you might like to include. Generally you should choose food that will cook quickly, although longer-cooking vegetables, such as pieces of carrot or potato can be left in the pot to simmer until cooked.

Arrange a choice of full-flavoured condiments: chopped chilli,

chilli sauce, crushed ginger or garlic, as well as sesame oil, hoisin sauce, lemon or lime juice, soy sauce or Guilin sauce. Give each diner a small plate so that they can mix the dipping sauce to their own tastes.

### TO COOK AND EAT:

Once the broth is boiling, reduce it to a simmer and take pieces of meat between your chopsticks, holding the strips in the bubbling broth. Each piece will cook in just a few seconds. It can then be dipped in the sauce and eaten immediately or placed in your bowl. Noodles can be cooked the same way or they may be added to the pot and scooped out later with chopsticks or a strainer, which is also useful for removing softer vegetables, dumplings and other foods. Eggs may be broken directly into the broth and allowed to poach until cooked.

Any remaining ingredients at the end of the meal may be added to the broth in the pot and cooked briefly. This makes a magnificent soup for the following day.

筷
子

# STEAMED TIBETAN MOMOS or CHINESE DUMPLINGS

Momos are very similar to Chinese wontons and other dumplings and you may decide if you want to cook the meat in the filling before steaming the filled dumplings. They may also be pan-fried instead of steaming, for about the same length of time, if preferred, taking care they do not stick, by adding a little more oil or water as necessary.

Mashed tofu or chopped and lightly sautéed vegetables such as cabbage, carrots, broccoli and herbs may be substituted for meat when serving vegetarians. A mix of well-spiced cooked potato filling makes an excellent samosa-like momo.

**Wrappers:**
1 cup flour
pinch of salt
water
vegetable, canola or sunflower cooking oil

**Filling:**
½ cup finely chopped onion
2 cloves of garlic, chopped finely
250g pork or other meat mince
1 tablespoon soy sauce
chilli sauce to taste
salt and freshly ground pepper to taste

Mix flour and salt, adding a little water at a time to make a stiff dough. Leave to stand while making filling.

Heat oil in a pan and fry onions until translucent. Add garlic and fry until just turning golden. Add the meat and cook until browning, then add soy and chilli sauces, mixing well. Season to taste and finish cooking the meat.

Divide the dough into equal-sized balls and roll into thin circles approximately 10cm in diameter, stretching the edges slightly to make them thinner than the centre.

Brush edges with water and place a tablespoon-full of filling in the centre. Fold each circle in half to make a semi-circle and pinch the edges firmly, pleating for an attractive effect. Small inexpensive plastic presses are available in Asian markets that will do this more easily. Place gently in a well-oiled steamer making sure the momos or dumplings do not touch, then steam for 10–15 minutes. Serve hot with chutney and a clear soup such as Thukpa for a Tibetan-style meal, or with any other broth or soup and dipping sauces.

**Serves 4**

筷子

## THUKPA

This soup may be made spicier by adding crushed chilli, and other vegetables such as potato, tomato and spinach can also be added. If using potatoes, cook them first or allow the soup to cook for longer.

2 tablespoons butter, ghee or cooking oil

2 cloves garlic, crushed

½ onion, finely chopped

4 cups chicken, beef or vegetable stock

salt or soya sauce and freshly ground pepper to taste

1 tablespoon grated ginger

2 eggs lightly beaten

1–2 cups fresh egg noodles, cooked

finely chopped coriander leaves, to garnish

Heat butter, ghee or oil in a large saucepan and fry garlic briefly, then add onion and cook until tender. Add stock, season to taste and add ginger, then simmer for ten minutes. Pour eggs into the soup and whisk well to break them into strands as they cook. Place some noodles in each bowl and pour the soup over them. Serve immediately with momos.

**Serves 4**

筷子

筷子

筷子

## PORTUGUESE TARTS

The key to this is rolling the pastry so it allows the flaky layers to show around the edge, and also cooking the tarts at a high heat.

3 egg yolks

½ cup castor sugar

2 tablespoons cornflour

1 cup cream

½ cup water

1 teaspoon grated lemon zest

2 teaspoons vanilla essence

1 sheet puff pastry, thawed

Whisk egg yolks, cornflour and sugar together in a bowl, then pour into a small saucepan set over a medium heat. Stir well, then slowly add cream and water, mixing until smooth. Add lemon zest, then heat, stirring constantly, just until the mixture boils. Remove immediately from the heat, stir in vanilla, and set aside to cool.

Tightly roll the sheet of pastry from the short side, then cut the rolled up pastry into 12 rounds. Lay rounds, cut-side up on a board and roll out each one into a 10cm circle. Press each circle into a muffin hole in a well-greased 12-hole pan. Strain custard and spoon enough into each pastry case to almost fill it. Bake in a preheated 220C oven for 20 minutes or until tops are blistered and very well-browned. Remove from trays and cool on racks.

**Makes 12**

## TOFFEE POTATOES

I couldn't believe my eyes when I first saw this dish. It sounds so unusual yet is quite delicious.

1kg potatoes
3–4 tablespoons cooking oil, butter or ghee
salt to taste
1 cup sugar
½ cup water

Peel potatoes and cut into quarters. Boil until tender then drain thoroughly. Heat oil, butter or ghee in a large heavy frypan and, when hot, add the potatoes, stirring until they are browning well. Season to taste with salt. Meanwhile make toffee by placing the sugar and water in a small heavy pan. Cook, over medium heat, stirring occasionally until it becomes golden. Place potatoes on individual plates or a serving dish and immediately pour some of the toffee lightly over the potatoes, enough so it is attractive but not so much as to form a hard shell. Think of using about the same amount as you would if generously sprinkling grated cheese over the dish.

**Serves 4**

筷
子

筷子

## CHILLI TOMATO EGGS

I have no idea what this dish is called in China, but we ate it from one side of the country to the other and it was delicious, and obviously very quick to prepare. While this recipe always appeared as part of a large selection of other dishes at the Chinese meals we ate, it would just as easily make a good breakfast dish or light meal.

    1–2 tablespoons peanut or other cooking oil
    1 onion, chopped
    1–2 cloves garlic, crushed
    1–2 small red chillies, according to taste, finely chopped
    ½ cup of corn kernels or peas (optional)
    4 tomatoes, chopped
    salt and freshly ground pepper to taste
    6 eggs, well beaten

Place the oil in a large heavy frypan and heat. Add onion and garlic and cook, stirring, until onions are translucent. Add chilli and stir well, then reduce heat immediately and add tomatoes, corn or peas, cooking slowly until well cooked. Season to taste. Pour eggs into the tomato mixture and cover the pan, stirring just a couple of times more to break the eggs up a little, cooking until set like scrambled eggs. Serve immediately.

**Serves 4**

筷子

# BRAISED FISH

This combination of frying and steaming retains every possible bit of flavour as well as preserving the moistness of the fish.

2 teaspoons grated fresh ginger

1 teaspoon sugar or honey

1 tablespoon soya sauce

1 tablespoon mirin

salt to taste

⅓ cup water

2 tablespoons oil

500g whole fish, scales removed, patted dry

pepper to taste

3 tablespoons chopped parsley or coriander

3 green onions, finely chopped

Mix ginger and sugar or honey. Add soya sauce, mirin, salt and water. Heat oil and brown fish on each side. Add sauce mixture, cover and cook for 10 minutes. Remove fish from the frypan and place on a dish that will fit in a steamer. Sprinkle pepper, parsley and spring onions over fish. Cover and steam 10 minutes, then serve with remaining sauce from the pan.

**Serves 2–4**

筷子

## FISH PORRIDGE OR CONGEE

Don't be put off by the name of this. You do not have to eat it for break-fast, although if you did, you would be well set up for the day. Think of it rather as a nutritious fish stew for any meal.

½ cup rice

2 tablespoons oil

6 cups water

300g firm white fish, thinly sliced

2 teaspoons soya sauce

1 teaspoon sesame oil

½ teaspoon salt (optional)

pepper to taste

1 cup dried rice vermicelli

oil to fry

6cm piece fresh ginger, shredded finely

1 green onion, finely chopped

1 tablespoon finely chopped coriander

Place rice and oil and water in a large saucepan. Allow to boil, then reduce heat and simmer for 1 1/2 hours. Marinate fish in a mixture of soya sauce, sesame oil, salt and pepper. Fry vermicelli in a little hot oil, drain and reserve until needed. Place boiling rice porridge in individual serving bowls. Top with fish slices and ginger. Garnish with green onions, coriander and pepper and fried vermicelli.

**Serves 4–6**

筷子

# STEAMED BUNS AND BLACK BEAN SAUCE

Almost any leftover or grated vegetables may be used in this recipe. It is the ideal opportunity to use up small amounts of leftovers in a really glamorous way. Canned black beans are usually very salted, so rinse them until they suit your own taste. The following recipe is meatless, but any minced meat or leftover cooked meat, finely chopped, is ideal to add as a filling.

### Dough:

1 cup plain white flour

1 teaspoon dry yeast

½ cup self raising flour

pinch salt

1 teaspoon oil

enough warm water to make dough

### Filling:

1 tablespoon peanut oil

2 tablespoons grated carrot

2 tablespoons finely grated oriental cabbage

2 tablespoons grated zucchini

1 tablespoon grated onion

1 teaspoon grated fresh ginger

1 clove garlic, crushed

1 tablespoon low-salt soya sauce

2 tablespoons ground roasted cashews

### Sauce:

¼ cup honey

¼ cup brown rice vinegar

1 cup chopped green onions

筷子

2 cloves garlic, crushed

2 teaspoons minced fresh ginger

1 tablespoon cornflour dissolved in 1 cup water

2 tablespoons canned black beans, rinsed to taste and mashed

Mix together flour, yeast, salt and oil in a medium bowl, adding just enough water to make a soft, springy dough. Knead lightly then place in a clean greased bowl, cover, and set aside for one hour while preparing filling.

Heat oil in a wok and add all filling ingredients except soya sauce and cashews. Stir-fry to combine, then place in a bowl and stir in soya sauce and cashews.

Take  walnut-sized pieces of dough and roll each out thinly to about 10cm diameter. Place a spoonful of filling in the centre of each piece, gather edges together and pinch firmly. Place filled rolls, seam side down in bamboo steamer and let stand for ½ an hour.

Put hot water in wok over medium heat. Set burner to medium heat, cover and steam for 20 minutes.

Place all sauce ingredients except beans in a saucepan and bring to the boil, stirring constantly. Add beans and serve with the buns when ready.

**Serves 4**

筷
子

# FISH CHOW MEIN

This dish is a real mixture of many delicious flavours. A complete meal-in-a-dish.

250g fine egg noodles

2cm knob fresh ginger, peeled and crushed

1 tablespoon soya sauce

1 tablespoon oil

500g firm white fish fillets, cut into 2cm squares

2 eggs

oil to fry

½ small cauliflower, thinly sliced

1 medium carrot, thinly sliced

6 dried shiitake mushrooms, soaked, drained, stems discarded, then thinly sliced

reserved soaking liquid from mushrooms

salt to taste

1 tablespoon cornflour

2 teaspoons soya sauce

½ teaspoon sesame oil

¼ teaspoon sugar (optional)

pepper to taste

Cook noodles for one minute in boiling salted water. Drain and set aside. Mix ginger, soy sauce and oil and marinate the fish in this for 15 minutes. Beat eggs and cook in a frypan or wok until set, like an omelette. Remove from pan and cut into strips. Heat more oil in the frypan, add noodles. Do not stir, but allow to form a 'cake'. Cook 3 minutes, each side. Drain. Saute vegetables and mushrooms for 2 minutes, then add 2 tablespoons reserved mushroom liquid and cook 1 minute. Pour over noodles. Mix cornflour, soya

筷子

sauce, ½ cup reserved mushroom liquid, sesame oil, sugar if using, and pepper together. Saute fish in a little oil until tender. Add sauce and cook until thickened. Pour over noodles and garnish with egg.

**Serves 4**

## BUTTER TEA

Of course in Tibet tea is made using yak butter and the mixture is pounded up and down by a plunger in a very tall cylinder. This way won't be the same, but it's fun to try it. Tibetans like their tea salty—that's right, salty—but make this to suit your own taste.

> 1 litre water
> 1 tablespoon tea leaves (Russian Caravan works well)
> 2 tablespoons cream
> 2 tablespoons milk
> 1 tablespoon butter
> salt

Boil the water and tea together in a saucepan for about 10 minutes. Strain off the tea leaves and add cream, milk and butter, then salt to taste. Reheat the tea if desired, but do not boil. If you like frothy tea, pour it backwards and forwards between two jugs.

**Makes 4 cups**

筷子

# CRISP SKIN FISH WITH SWEET AND SOUR SAUCE

This is a special dish as it looks so glamorous and colourful.

750g whole snapper, cleaned and scaled, but with head and
tail left on

½ teaspoon salt

½ teaspoon five spice powder

oil to fry

1 egg, beaten

¼ cup cornflour

**Sauce:**

1 carrot, thinly sliced

3 tablespoons frozen or fresh peas

1 tablespoon light soya sauce

1 tablespoon mirin

3 tablespoons tomato sauce or puree

2 tablespoons vinegar

2 tablespoons sugar or honey

¾ cup water

1 tablespoon cornflour

3 tablespoons cold water

2 tablespoons peanut oil

2 cloves, garlic, crushed

½ teaspoon finely grated fresh ginger

1 small onion, cut in wedges

2 tablespoons mango, sliced (optional)

Wash fish well and wipe dry. Slash skin diagonally on each side,
several times in opposite directions to make diamond shapes. Mix salt
and five spice powder together and rub into fish skin and slashes.

筷
子

Make sauce by bringing a little water to the boil, then adding carrots and peas. Cook one minute, drain, then drop into cold water. Combine soya sauce, mirin, tomato sauce or puree, vinegar, sugar or honey and water and stir to dissolve sugar. Mix cornflour with the cold water. Heat oil and add garlic, ginger, peas, carrots and onion. Fry 2 minutes. Add sauce mixture, bring to the boil, then carefully add dissolved cornflour. Stir until thickened, then add mango if using. Keep warm while frying fish.

Heat 2cm oil in a large frypan, large enough for the fish, and deep enough so there is no splattering of oil. Dip fish in egg then cornflour. Fry fish for approximately 4 minutes on each side, or until cooked through. Drain, place on a serving platter and spoon a little sauce over. Accompany with a bowl of sauce passed separately.

**Serves 4**

筷子

## CHICKEN FILLED CHINESE MUSHROOMS

If Chinese mushrooms are unavailable, use large fresh mushrooms.

32 large Chinese (shiitake) mushrooms, soaked for 30 minutes in hot water, drained and stems discarded

1 cup chicken mince

½ teaspoon shrimp paste

1 small onion, chopped

1 tablespoon cornflour

1 egg

1 tablespoon each soy sauce and mirin

**Sauce**

1 cup chicken stock

1 tablespoon cornflour

1 teaspoon sesame seed oil

1 teaspoon soy sauce

Match mushrooms into equal-sized pairs. Mix chicken mince, shrimp paste, onion, cornflour, egg, mirin and soy sauce in a bowl. Mound one tablespoonful into the caps of half the mushrooms. Top with remaining mushrooms. Press well together. Steam 20–30 minutes. Make sauce by dissolving cornflour in a little chicken stock. Heat remaining stock and other ingredients until boiling. Stir in dissolved cornflour and cook, stirring, until thickened. Pour over mushrooms and serve very hot.

**Makes 16**

筷子

筷子

筷子